STANDARD GUIDE TO BUILDING

Street Rods

AND CUSTOM CARS

HOW TO GET THE MOST CAR FOR YOUR MONEY

KEN WICKHAM

Published by

700 East State Street • Iola, WI 54990-0001
715/445-2214 • FAX: 715/445-4087   www.krause.com

Please call or write for our free catalog.
Our toll-free number to place an order or obtain a free catalog is 800-258-0929.

Library of Congress Catalog Number: 2002105092
ISBN: 0-87349-441-5

Printed in the United States of America

To my father, Kenneth Wickham,
and my mother, Beverly Wickham,
who were there every step of the way.

Contents

(courtesy of Kemp's Rod and Restoration)

(courtesy of Street Rods by Michael)

(courtesy of Gibbon Fiberglass Reproductions)

Introduction

I started my "education" in cars by serving as an apprentice for a shop that restored high-point show cars. Every nut and bolt had to be perfect. Every aspect of the car was restored so that it resembled a time capsule. You literally stepped back in time to see a car exactly the way it would have rolled off the assembly line. I spent years perfecting my craft and even branched off and ran my own shop. I attended and lectured at many shows, but there always seemed to be something missing.

Somewhere towards the end of the last millennium I found myself speaking in front of a crowd that was mostly full of street rod and custom car enthusiasts. Naturally, the group could really care less about what kind of trivial stamping was found on the head of some bolt. They were mostly interested in what new techniques I offered in the world of paint. But this group rubbed off on me. For the first time in years I felt relaxed at a car show and that's when it hit me: This car show was different. When I came home, I found myself dwelling on the event and my friends were asking me what was different about the show. I guess if I had to summarize the street rod and custom car world in one word, it would have to be "fun."

The cars are fun and the people are fun, but there is a lot more. Everybody at the show is there to have a good time. It's relaxing. It's creative. There are no boundaries. If you feel like painting the grill and bumpers — go ahead, do it. What's stopping you? There really aren't any rules. Everything is an opinion or personal taste and I love the freedom of custom cars.

But don't believe what you see from Hollywood when it comes to street rods. There are several movies that include old cars in the plot, and the stories are very similar: the main character is somehow an outcast, he finds an old car in a field, spends a couple of weekends working real hard, wipes the grease off his forehead and wins the heart of the most beautiful girl in town. The building of the car usually takes five minutes of the movie or so and gives the impression that building cars is easy and can be done quickly.

Did you ever see the movie "Christine?" I'm the worst one to take to a movie like that because I'm the knucklehead in the back row screaming, "Hey, where did he paint that thing anyway?" "Hey, how did some high school kid pay for the chrome?" Cars take time, so if you are still thinking that you are going to buy this old car in the field, put about 40 hours of hard work into it and sell the car for a profit, then I hope this book will provide a dose of reality. It doesn't happen that way

with point show cars and it most certainly doesn't happen with custom cars.

This book will help you plan — the lack of a good plan is the most common reason for failed projects. It's the reason why you see so many ads where people are selling unfinished cars. "Must sell — 90 percent complete — like new — rare find!" This failure can be avoided with a well-thought-out plan.

The second reason for failure is unrealistic expectations. The first example that comes to mind is the whole 40-hour "Hollywood" thing. It just doesn't happen that way. You should expect to commit 1,000 to 2,000 hours on a custom project, and that takes years, not weeks.

This hobby also takes money, but you do have control over how much. This book will talk about how to set a budget and then plan towards that budget. No high school kid is going to lay down a show car in six weeks working minimum wage and 10 hours a week. It just isn't possible!

Another bubble that I need to burst is the whole myth that you're going to sell this car for a profit and quit your day job. You're just going to have to trust me at this point, but custom automotive work at best will only be worth the sum of its parts.

The very definition of custom car means that this car is special to YOU. The probability that someone will desire every exact detail that matched your personal desires is very low, which means the car's greatest value lies with you. No need to beat a dead horse here, but stick to coin collecting if you're into the money, but continue in your journey with custom cars if you simply love old cars like I do. You wouldn't go to a theme park expecting to make a profit would you? The money is something you pay for the fun!

Safety! OK, Mrs. Fort, my old English teacher, wouldn't approve of me writing a one-word sentence, but safety is very important. I'm going to discuss a whole bunch of really cool, destructive tools. I can relate to the whole "Home Improvement" TV show. I love loud tools that tear stuff up, but you know what? You don't have to be missing fingers or have a dog with a patch over its eye to be cool.

I've worked with people with missing eyes and fingers. Cars fall off blocks, too. In fact, a friend of the family is no longer with us because he was under a car when it happened, and he left his widow six kids to support. Then there is all the slow agonizing stuff like only having one lung or cancer of the liver. We use a lot of chemicals in this hobby and they require special care to use. Once again, I'm not trying to discourage you, but safety procedures are very important. If someone has experience at something, it doesn't mean that they are good, it just means that they have learned from a lot of mistakes. These are the gruesome mistakes you really want to avoid.

Finally, one of the most exciting aspects of this book, hopefully, is that you will be exposed to a mountain of information. Following are numerous resources for parts and the appendix at the end of the book is excellent. At your fingertips will be countless contacts for parts and labor. If you're not on the Internet by now, take the leap of faith and get there. The Web can be perhaps the most important single ally for the automotive enthusiast. I can find a part in hours in what used

to take me months. It's awesome!

However, what I am most excited about is something I don't think I have ever seen in a book like this. I have interviewed dozens of established experts in the street rod and custom world and have condensed their knowledge into the pages of this book. We'll drift from shop to shop around the country and see how mechanics and body men tackle problems differently. There will be times where there really isn't a right way to do something and instead of being exposed to just one point of view, we'll see several angles.

This book will hopefully save you time, money and headaches. We are about to step into a world with no boundaries. I'm really excited, and I hope you are, too.

(courtesy of Kemps Rod and Restoration)

Chapter 1

How Did Hot Rodding Begin?

I remember wandering the halls of a hot rod show at the Astrodome in Houston, Texas, one summer. As I gazed at the hundreds of cars around me, I couldn't help but wonder: "How and where did this phenomenon begin? Who was responsible? Who built the first hot rod and why?" It turns out the answer isn't very simple.

Several events throughout time were necessary to create the possibility of a hot rod. The first, obviously, had to be the invention of the automobile itself, and there were actually many inventors involved in its creation. "Cars" can be traced all the way back to the early 1800s. Actually, they were massive, steam-driven monsters that looked more like large tractors than cars. They weren't even close to practical and were so heavy they would bog down in the crude dirt roads of the time.

Ever heard of a Stanley Steamer? Well, the Stanley brothers were building steam-powered cars as late as the 1920s. Steam engines were big, heavy and difficult to maintain. A new power plant was needed to make cars more practical and we have Nicolaus Otto to thank for it. He invented and built the first four-stroke internal combustion engine and called it the "Otto Cycle Engine."

(From the Collections of Henry Ford Museum & Greenfield Village)

The Quadricycle was the first car Henry Ford built. Shown here in 1910 on Broadway in New York, this car was already 14 years old and running fine.

This photo of Henry Ford's "999 Racer" with Ford and driver, Barney Oldfield, was taken in 1901. Note the steering handle and massive radiator.

He didn't have it long before he stuck it on a bicycle and made one of the world's first practical motorcycles.

Americans take a lot of pride in their inventions and there have been many. I seem to recall being told in grade school that Henry Ford invented the first automobile and that Americans were responsible for bringing cars to the world, but I'm afraid that is not true. Ford was both instrumental and fundamental to the hot rod industry, but he did not invent the car. Essentially, there were hundreds, if not thousands, of inventors all over the world tinkering around with engines, bicycles and carriages. Many of these people were oceans apart and working on the same invention simultaneously and completely unaware of what others were doing.

ONCE UPON A TIME ...

Generally, historians look to the person who filed the first patent to be the first inventor. If that is the case, the first person to file a patent for a gas-fueled car was German Karl Benz in 1886. His first car really looked like a large, three-wheeled motorcycle, so if you ever broke your arm on a three-wheeler as a kid, you have this man to thank for it. By 1900, his company, Benz & Cie, was the largest manufacturer of automobiles in the world.

The first American inventor of the gas-powered engine was John Lambert in 1891 — two years before Henry Ford. Ford was working for Thomas Edison at the time, but started tinkering with engines and in 1893 he successfully built his first engine. Picture this image,

he ran his first engine in the kitchen sink! His wife must have been a tolerant woman, because something tells me he didn't have a muffler on that thing.

His neighbors called him "Crazy Henry" for what appeared to be an obsession with the horseless carriage. Ford worked a normal job for Thomas Edison by day and labored by night in his shed. He was truly a man possessed by his creativity, and in the middle of the night in June of 1896, he finished his first car. There was just one problem: He was so focused on the day-to-day building of the car, that he never bothered to check if it would even fit out the door of his shed and sure enough it was too wide. No problem for Ford, however, he just grabbed a sledgehammer and "made" the door wider! Can you see him at 2 in the morning bashing a hole in the wall of his shed?

By 1901, Ransom Olds made the first real bid to mass produce automobiles, but his car was too fragile to withstand the American landscape and never really caught on. There were at least 30 American auto manufacturers at the turn of the century and it is at this time that some of the first "hot rodding" took place. Cars were still thought of as "freakish" and manufacturers sought out racing as a means to prove roadworthiness to potential customers and pick up some free publicity. However, Ford was a racer before he was a businessman and was actively building racecars at the turn of the century. In 1901, he entered one of them in a race at Grosse Pointe, Michigan, and won. This win caught

The Model T was the first affordable family car. Twenty-plus years later, it started becoming a test vehicle for the earliest amateur hot rodders.

(From the Collections of Henry Ford Museum & Greenfield Village)

the eye of an investor and together they formed the Ford Motor Company in 1903.

It is the years between 1903-1908 that the foundation for hot rodding became possible. I know that most people in the industry will say hot rodding got started after WWII on a salt flat, but that is just too simplistic.

Hot rods were not the fancy, highly buffed, pretty cars they are today. They were speed machines built on tight budgets, and these mechanics never would have had access to inexpensive parts if it wasn't for Ford and the ideas coming out of his company at this point in history. During the early years, Ford battled with stockholders for the direction of the company. The company first built expensive, highly profitable cars. This may have made the stockholders happy, but he insisted that the future lay with an inexpensive, high-volume solution.

THE FORD REVOLUTION

If things hadn't changed, we may have never seen the rise of the Ford Company, but a little luck was about to shine on Henry Ford. First. His partner and primary investor ran into financial trouble, which eventually allowed Ford to gain a majority share of stock in his company. Once he had control of the stock he was able to carry out his own ideas. The second event that worked in Ford's favor was an economic crash in 1907. I know we don't usually think of a crash as a good thing, but this downward trend in the economy helped convince many stockholders to give Ford's ideas a try. Ford had been pressing for inexpensive, low-margin cars all along; but without these "lucky" events, it's possible Ford would have disappeared with so many other manufacturers in the Great Depression of the 1930s.

Prior to 1908, cars were hand built and produced in small numbers. They were expensive and unreliable.

They were not considered a replacement for the horse at the turn of the century. Instead, cars were toys or gadgets for the idle rich. Many people that owned cars actually had a full-time mechanic on the payroll and usually drove their cars with the mechanic by their side. It was just easier to use a horse.

Ford's Model T was different. He sat down and designed a car with newer, simplified parts. The cars were reliable, inexpensive to produce and had a simple design that was easy to put together (and easy to take apart — hint, hint). Just in case any of you ever end up on a talk show, the Model T was the first American car to use a new kind of steel called vanadium steel (invented by the French). This new steel was lighter and stronger than any other in its time.

Ford kept the options and the choices to a minimum and finally put the build process on an assembly line. All of this controlled costs and led to a low-cost automotive solution that was somewhat reliable. Ford designed the Model T in secret with only a select few of the employees even knowing it existed. One could argue that this was done to avoid industrial espionage, but the more likely reason was to avoid headaches from investors and board members.

It took Ford two years to design, but in 1908, he revealed to the world his little black Model T and asked $850 for it. The car initially was not built on an assembly line, however; it was built in little workstations where a small team of workers put the entire cars together. Ford sold a staggering 10,000 Model Ts in its first year. In 1912, the Model T price was reduced to $575 and, for the first time in history, the automobile actually was less than the average annual U.S. wage. By 1913, the process changed so that the entire car was built on a conveyer and the first complete automotive assembly line was born. The price quickly dropped to $290 over the next few years.

He used rather ingenious marketing methods — one of the more humorous was a tour of Model T rodeos where drivers riding in Fords tried to rope cattle. Fords were actually winning endurance races around the country, including the first transcontinental race of 1909. Ford was able to capture the publicity of the win, even though his modified Model T was later disqualified when officials learned that the engine was changed during the race. Either way, only three cars actually finished the race and two of those were modified Model Ts. Ford's reliability proved to be a powerful marketing tool and the word was spreading that these Model Ts could someday replace the horse!

Ford is generally credited with implementing the first assembly line, which led to mass production. Actually, Ford borrowed the assembly line idea after he took a trip to Chicago once and toured the famous Chicago meat-packing plants. The beef carcasses would travel on an overhead trolley and each butcher would remove their specific cut of beef and push the carcass on to the next butcher. In effect, this was a non-motorized "disassembly" line.

Ford started introducing automation in his factory in 1910 and tinkered with it every day. The task before him was staggering. No two portions of a car take the exact same time to build. Take the chassis for example. The frames would have to be put in jigs and riveted or welded together, then passed on to the next station. There, a worker would add the first foundation parts, like suspension, and then pass it on. This would continue until there was a finished chassis and it would pass on down the line for body assembly.

The problem that Ford had to tackle concerned the timing of the line. For example, it's a lot easier and faster to bolt leaf springs on a frame than it is to build the frame itself, so you ended up with some workers sitting around waiting for the next task. He eventually solved this problem with trial and error, old-fashioned hard work and sheer genius.

MAKE WAY FOR THE MODEL A

OK, so what does all this history stuff have to do with hot rods? Well, Henry Ford and his company were so efficient that by 1927, 15 million Model Ts had been produced, which represented half of the cars in existence at the time. Trouble had been brewing, though. Chevrolet had been steadily eroding Model T sales. Drivers could get more amenities for a similar low price and the writing was on the wall that the Model T needed to be changed. Henry Ford would hear nothing of it and insisted the Model T was here to stay. It took the constant nagging of his son and a rapid drop in sales in 1927 to convince him otherwise.

Ford then provided an example of what not to do when transitioning a factory to something new. Ford quickly decided that a new model was needed, so he shut down the plant, sent all the workers home, and they stayed there for six months! He and his team of engineers designed the new model and ramped up the assembly line for the next great thing — the Model A. Keep in mind, there was no vast network of used car sales at the time. Many people just kept the old Ts as a second car or retired them to a barn.

So at this point in history we find America in an economic boom, 15 million Model Ts on the roads and

The Model A replaced the Model T in 1929 and marked the first great step in automobile evolution in the United States.

By the 1930s, Model Ts began collecting dust and rust in many backyards. Many got second lives as hot rods, but this beautiful 1913 version survived intact.

a brand new model essentially making all of these older cars obsolete. Several million more Model As were produced in just the four years between 1928 and 1932. If you include all the manufacturers, there were more than 30 million obsolete cars floating around the country with no real value.

The U.S. government actually considered this a great problem. The great stock market crash of 1929 led to a massive depression and new car sales plummeted. In the years that followed, the majority of America's several hundred auto manufacturers either went out of business or merged with each other due to low sales volume. Many of the Model T cars were built so well that they were running fine well into the 1930s, so many Americans opted to hold off on buying a new car until things got better. The U.S. government decided that the solution to ending the depression was to get people to buy goods again, so the government started destroying huge surpluses of goods in the hopes that it would force people to buy things again. Most of the destruction centered on agriculture, but cars were not immune. There are numerous photos of tall Model T bonfires. Of course, no recycling was authorized. The goal of this exercise was to get manufacturers to buy new steel, too. The photos are somewhat disturbing, but the good news is that there were so many cars produced that the government didn't come close to making

a dent in the surplus of old cars. If they had, the story of the hot rod would have been much different.

PICKING UP SPEED

By 1932 advanced technology was on the way — like the V8 engine. Car manufacturers started boasting claims of stock car speeds in excess of 70 mph! This ultimately lays another brick in our hot rod foundation — America's need for speed. It's difficult to say who built the first hot rod. One could argue that those 1901 speedsters Henry Ford raced on were hot rods, but a more accepted definition for hot rod is "any pre-1949 car that has been modified to gain speed."

If you have an interest in early hot rod history, I highly recommend reading the book *Hot Rod Magazine: The First 12 Issues.*" Several clues to the origin of hot rods can be found in these first issues of the magazine. The majority of the photos center on oval-track racing and not the speed records of the Bonneville Salt Flats. Another interesting note of the early years can be found in the ads themselves. You don't find the term "hot rod" used in the commercial ads. Instead, you see the term "speed" used where we use the term custom or street rod today. Many of the advertisements feature "speed shops" or "speed parts."

Early hot rodding was not about *American Graffiti* Saturday night cruising or fancy car shows, but more about racing and setting land speed records. Of course, no magazine would be complete without a "Hot Rod of the Month" page or pictures of women posing with car parts. It had a *Playboy* feel about it, even though it was a good six years before that magazine came along. Most of the cars are not painted, and are very rough by today's standards. However, one thing is clear: By the time the magazine was first issued in 1948, a whole hot rodding industry already existed.

BORN ON THE BACK ROADS

So when did hot rods first hit the streets and why? Well, we have to take a guess at the why, but there are pictures of crude hot rods all the way back to the '30s. Our best guess of the "why" revolves around friendship and competition. It's likely that the first hot rods were only slightly modified and were used as a low-cost source of entertainment for young men around the country.

Picture this scenario: Two pals from high school have several things in common. Their parents both have 20-year-old Model Ts sitting in the barn collecting dust, both have limited budgets and both have free time on their hands after school and chores. Every weekend these pals would race around the rural dirt roads of the day and every week each would learn some new trick. It wasn't long before engine modifications were being made and excess sheet metal was removed to pick up extra speed. This scenario was not unusual. After all, some locations around the country didn't have electricity, let alone movie theaters or other forms of entertainment. Amateur racing was fun and people all over the country were discovering it. As more people got involved in the "speed" hobby, small dirt tracks were built to provide a safe place for people to race.

Why spend so much time discussing Henry Ford? Well, by the 1930s you had millions of aging, obsolete and "extra" vehicles around just waiting to be tinkered with. The extra cars were a great source of cheap parts, too. By the time World War II started, the hot rod industry had already set roots, but soon everyone, both male and female, had a job to do and there wasn't much extra time to tinker with hot rods. Even though the war may have put a halt to hot rodding initially, it actually added fuel to the fire. You almost couldn't be involved in that war without picking up some mechanical skills.

Many observers have said that the war was won by the mobility the jeep offered. If you were in a tank, jeep or truck that broke down, you couldn't pull over to the side of the road and wait for a wrecker. It was in a soldier's best interest to pick up a few mechanical skills and get your vehicle going yourself.

By 1946, most Americans had been deprived of a new car for four years or more, so the demand for new vehicles skyrocketed after the war. A surge of post war car buying began, which resulted in the retirement of all the '30s coupes and sedans. Remember all of those factory claims of 70 mph stock coupes? What would happen if we took one of those old cars, hopped up the engine, beefed up the suspension and shed off all the extra weight? All we needed were those extra, now inexpensive V8 engines to complete the puzzle.

So let's recap. Through the introduction of mass production, there were literally millions of scrap vehicles available for parts at near "giveaway" prices. We had road tracks for safe racing peppered all over the country and new ones were being built all the time. There was a surplus of powerful engines that were easy to work on and a nation full of young mechanics looking for something to do. The growth of the hot rod was inevitable.

Model As, like this 1929 Phaeton, made the Model T obsolete, but they eventually turned into hot rod fodder themselves.

Chapter 2

Developing a Plan

Now I don't want to come across like I'm giving a father-in-law speech, but perhaps the most important question I could ask you is "What is your plan?" When I read books, I'm bad about skipping the introduction; and if some of you have the same bad habits, you may have missed a very important point: Don't even pick up a wrench without having a plan! If you already started this project, then stop! I need to emphasize that the primary reason for failed custom projects is a lack of planning.

So where do we start? Well, we start with the most obvious question first: What kind of custom car are we going to build? I teach seminars at trade shows and such. I can't tell you how many people come up afterwards to ask questions and their entire plan is sketched out on a napkin! "And ... you already mailed out checks and started spreading your credit card around buying parts with this? This napkin is your plan?" Guys like that give me an ulcer.

So many people start with a sketch or a picture of what the car will look like and start picking color options from day one with no plan. Have you set a budget? Do you know how much time you will spend on this? How much will you do yourself?

WHAT KIND OF CAR?

Your plan should be a folder of information and our first step is choosing the car's style. This is an important step and some serious thought should go into this. We need to study all the different styles, address their difficulty, and discuss how expensive they are to build. Let's start this process with the cars that are the easiest and least expensive to build and work up.

The cars that come first are actually the ones that come first in hot rodding history. This makes sense because these first hot rods were built on low budgets by pioneers of the industry. The first two types of hot rods were roadsters and streamliners. Both of these are cool-looking cars that are fairly easy to build and would be great beginner cars.

ROADSTERS

The roadster was generally a '20s or '30s Ford that had all the unnecessary sheet metal removed and improvements made to the engine and suspension. They were almost always open road cars with no roof, fenders or engine cowl. Many of them had Model T bodies with nothing but the radiator out front. This was

This car has hidden door handles and hinges. This fiberglass body came from the manufacturer that way, but metal cars will have to be altered to achieve this look.

(courtesy of Street Rods by Michael)

Notice the car's rake. This is the angle caused by the larger tires in the rear. This car is built for speed, not necessarily Saturday night cruising.

(courtesy of Street Rods by Michael)

the easiest car to build and is the most common car you see in the old issues of *Hot Rod Magazine*. These first cars were not exactly attractive in the sense the interiors were stripped and they lacked paint, but they were fast. In today's market, you would expect this type of car to have both beautiful paint and interior work along with several other modern amenities, like fuel injection, disc brakes and stereo equipment.

This style of car is frequently what comes to mind when people think of a "hot rod," but it could also be called a "high boy" or "street rod." A very nice version of this can be built in a budget of $20,000, with that price coming down if you do more work yourself. I highly recommend that your first car fall into this category. This may not be what you sketched on that napkin, but it's a good idea to start with something simple and work your way up as you learn.

STREAMLINERS

The other type of early hot rod was called the "streamliner," and this style is very rare today. This was essentially a racecar with sheet metal wrapped around the driver and enclosing the engine compartment to reduce drag. Sometimes mechanics would build these out of old drop tanks from WWII fighters and most of the first speed records were made in streamliners. The problem with them is they only seat one person, which is fine for racing but isn't exactly fun on a Saturday night. I guess a modern equivalent would be today's Formula 1 and Indy cars. Since streamliners are not exactly practical, I will be spending very little time talking about building them.

"STREET RODS"

"Street rod" is a newer term and it covers any custom car built before 1949. The definition is similar to hot

rod and most people use the terms interchangeably. There are some hot rod clubs that are Ford specific, but street rod clubs are all encompassing and welcome all makes. You would expect to see some roadsters and high boys at a street rod show, but the majority of the cars are enclosed with a chopped roof and have most of their original sheet metal, like the fenders and hood. They usually have the trim and bumpers removed with an array of paint schemes and interior styles. This is very much a free form vehicle built with an "anything goes" approach. Street rods usually have an intact body that seats four and are not much more difficult to build than the hot rod roadsters.

Their cost varies from the same $20,000 to outrageous, depending on the modifications made. Typically the national show winners have a good $150,000 in them and tour the national show circuit. The shows generally require some kind of display and most of these cars travel in a full-length tractor-trailer rig. You can build a very nice street rod in the $20,000 to $40,000 price range.

"CUSTOM" CRUISERS

Every car mentioned so far is a custom car. Custom only implies that changes have been made to alter the car from stock. The term "custom" is used for everything under the sun. However, when I hear the term "custom," I usually think of a '50s or '60s car built for cruising. After all, if the hot rod industry got started to fulfill the need for speed, the custom or "kustom" industry began to express individuality. Most people in the industry have then taken the word "kustom" to describe this era of Saturday night cruisers. These cars are large, heavy, time consuming and fairly costly to build.

One type of custom car is a modified or semi-modified style. These cars are essentially stock with just a

This Mustang is essentially stock, with the exception of the paint. One change like the color of the paint from original, will send a car to the semi-modified class, but it takes much more to be a true custom.

few changes. I won't spend a lot of time addressing this class of vehicle because they do not have much customization. I recommend staying 100 percent original or going full custom, but a stock car with one change like mag wheels just looks odd.

THE LEAD SLED

Custom cars include the "lead sled" varieties. Custom cars hit the scene in the late 1940s and '50s and many of the people involved were hot rodders. Some people enjoyed working on cars but just didn't have an interest

in racing. Many of the first custom techniques involved paint. I have always thought that flames came first and scallops followed decades later, but I have now seen examples of simple scallop designs back in the '40s, which leads me to believe scallops came first and morphed into flames during the '50s. Every time someone thought of something new like candied paint or flames, it wasn't long before everyone was following suit, so people looked at the body itself to find originality.

Some of the first modifications centered on cleaning the factory-built lines. Bumpers, mirrors, door handles

As the car models move past 1948 and into the '50s and '60s the terminology describing them changes to kustom, custom and lead sled, to name just a few. These cars will be the most expensive to build for several reasons. Most of these cars are 18 feet or longer and that adds to the paint and bodywork expense. There are several thousand more parts on these cars than what you find on Model As, so the man hours to handle and replace all of these parts jumps considerably. The factory packed these cars with chrome and decorative trim. Chrome plating has increased in price to the point where some owners have found plating to be the single highest cost in the entire project. A 1950s custom show car can have $30,000 in chrome or more. This '49 Caddy has almost flawless paint and bodywork. A show car of this size can run more than $100,000 to build with the more normal street customs running more $40,000.

(courtesy of Street Rods by Michael)

This fiberglass-bodied coupe represents one of the most common street rod styles. Fiberglass has become the new standard for hot rods now that metal donor cars have all but disappeared.

and chrome decorations came off. It wasn't until people started grafting the parts from one car into another before the word "lead" comes into the picture. Whenever you take an external part, like a taillight, and sink it into the body so that it fits flush, you have a process called "frenching." Frenched lights give the car a very sleek, clean appearance, but require welding on the skin of the body to pull off properly.

In the '40s and '50s, you didn't have polyester fillers like Bondo available, so people used lead to fill in the welds and low spots. By the time you french in all the exterior parts, chop the top, and even modify the shape

of the body; you end up with quite a bit of lead on the car and hence the term "lead sled."

LOWERING AND CHANNELING

Some customizers were not satisfied with the height of their cruiser, so they looked for ways to lower the car to the ground. The first efforts at this involved cutting links out of the front coil springs and removing leafs out of the rear, but this decreased performance and proved dangerous in some cases. Along comes channeling. Channeling can be time consuming; but what happens is the customizer removes the metal on

One of the most desirable custom cars is the early '50s Merc. Many people think that scalloped paint jobs are a modern design. Actually, there are photos of scalloped paint jobs on the earliest hot rods and it is believed that this design evolved into flames as time went on.

The Mercury "Merc" is possibly the pinnacle of custom cars. This classic lead sled has been lowered, had its roof chopped and turn signals frenched. Very little is stock on a car like this. The metal work on the roof alone is complicated and takes extreme skill. Don't count on getting out of a project like this cheaply.

(courtesy of Kemp's Rod and Restoration)

the floor that is in contact with the frame, lowers the body in relation to the ground and welds the floor back up. Frenching and channeling are not tasks for the novice. They are time consuming, and in this business, time equals big money.

KNOW WHAT YOU'RE GETTING INTO

Proper budgeting is key to a good plan and as I walk you through the steps in the next chapters, I will point out what certain parts and labor cost. I recommend that you set a budget first, read the chapters thoroughly and

then decide what you will need to do yourself to stick to your budget.

For example, if you set a budget for $5,000, a nice car can still be made, but you will need to learn every skill involved, including all mechanical, body, paint and interior work. To pull it off, you'll be getting parts out of junkyards, painting parts instead of chroming them, painting the car in your garage and stitching the interior yourself. I have been doing this for years and still wouldn't try to do everything myself. Being realistic with your skills assessment also leads to a good plan and a

(courtesy of Kemp's Rod and Restoration)

This street rod would be a high boy if it lacked fenders and running boards. Notice the oversized tires at the rear and lack of door and trunk handles. These features have become the norm.

This '56 Merc has had some trim removed for a simple, but dramatic, effect. The trim design gives the car a modern feel. Planning is needed to know which trim mounting holes will need to be welded and which ones left.

higher probability of success. Building a street rod for less than $10,000 is extremely difficult to do.

The good news is that this is the very definition of planning. Read the entire book, select the type of custom car you like, budget the parts, materials and labor, and methodically act out your plan step by step. You do as much work as you feel comfortable with and get a professional to do the rest. I highly recommend surfing the Web and looking at the endless supply of custom car photos. Thousands of people have posted their e-mail addresses online and you can start networking with people who have been down the same road. Keep a folder with all your contacts and start pricing parts and asking questions. If you struggle with creating the car's concept, there are artists that are experienced with custom cars that can help you draw up a concept and paint scheme. They are reasonably priced.

One page on Michael Young's Web site is extremely helpful during planning: http://www.srbymichael.com /arc.shtml. I recommend visiting this site and looking for a car you like. The site breaks down more than a dozen models by price. The following is one example found on this site. Your plan should include a price breakout similar to this one.

Gibbon - '32 3 Window Full-Fendered

BODY			
	Body - Gibbon -'32 - 3 window coupe - 2 inch chop.	$6,700.00	
	BODY FEATURES: Filled cowl & top, complete floor, wood reinforced w/top bows, package tray w/rear window box, interior garnish moldings, doors hung & latched, deck lid hung, trans tunnel cover, steel cowl brace, recessed firewall.		
	FREE OPTIONS: Stock or hidden hinges, stock or smooth dash, trunk or rumble seat.		
	OPTIONS		
	Power window installed w/side & rear tinted glass.	$600.00	
	Body package - Four fenders, front splash apron, grill shell, pair of rear horn covers, pair of running boards (smooth or stock)	$1,200.00	
	Glass - front - tinted	$200.00	
	Head lights, bar, conduit, w/pads & bolts	$254.00	
	Parking & turn signal lights	UPGRADE	$20.00
	Specialty wipers w/intermediate	UPGRADE	$300.00
	Tail lights pair - '39 Ford blue dot w/pads	UPGRADE	$76.00
	Grill insert	$250.00	
	Hood -3 or 4 piece complete (scoops or louvers option)	$550.00	
	Hood prop, bars, brackets bumper kit & center - 4 piece hood only.	UPGRADE	$111.00
	Outside handles - door & deck lid	UPGRADE	$82.25
	Power trunk lift	UPGRADE	$190.00
	Radiator splash apron hardware kit	$10.00	
	Front fender braces & running board braces	$130.00	
	TOTAL	**$9,894.00**	
FRAME			
	Stage 3 Chassis - complete	$6,578.00	
	Fully boxed frame - front & rear crossmember, tube center, manual brake pedal assembly and master cylinder - Vega mount, complete 4 bar front end or hair pin with axle, spring, spring perches, spring shackles, steering arms, spindles, shocks, u-bolt, lower shock mounts, king pins, tie rod with ends, brackets welded in place, front brake kit, drag link, pitman arm, front panhard bar, Vega steering box, Ford 9" rear end narrowed with axles, bearings, rear brakes, backing plates, third member rebuilt (275,300,325), rear coil over shocks, triangular 4 bar or parallel 4 bar*, all brackets welded in place. *Parallel 4 bar need rear panhard bar - see Options for price*		
	Stage 3 Chassis - complete - as above SS - GM brakes	UPGRADE	$1,019.00
	Hi-tech disc brake upgrade for straight axle	UPGRADE	$1,619.00
	IFS standard - GM brakes	UPGRADE	$486.00
	IFS SS - GM brakes - includes rear 4 bar upgrade to SS	UPGRADE	$1,014.00

	IFS show custom disc brakes includes rear 4 bar upgrade to SS	UPGRADE	$1,241.00
	IFS show Hi-tech disc brakes - includes rear 4 bar upgrade SS	UPGRADE	$1,541.00
	Power brakes w/master cylinder & booster	UPGRADE	$369.00
	Steel brake lines w/residual valves & proportionate valve	$300.00	
	SS brake lines w/residual valves & proportionate valve	UPGRADE	$300.00
	Drive shaft	$300.00	
	Emergency brake, cables, & boot - Lokar	UPGRADE	$195.00
	Fuel lines	$30.00	
	Front & rear SS spreader bars	$125.00	
	Poly gas tank w/cover	$275.00	
	Gas tank - SS - Rock Valley	UPGRADE	$275.00
	TOTAL	**$7,608.00**	
ENGINE			
	Crate engine - SBC 210 HP	$1,700.00	
	Crate engine - SBC 300 HP	UPGRADE	$1,000.00
	Crate engine - SBC 355 HP	UPGRADE	$2,000.00
	Brackets - Alan Grove alternator	$70.00	
	Brackets - Billet Specialties polished A/C/Alt.	UPGRADE	$130.00
	Pulleys - Chevrolet stock steel pulleys	$80.00	
	Pulleys - Billet Specialties V-belt polished	UPGRADE	$60.00
	Alternator - 100 amp - chrome	$124.00	
	Water pump - plain SW	$35.00	
	Water pump - Tuff-Stuff chrome SW	UPGRADE	$60.00
	Starter - plain	$75.00	
	Starter - PowerMaster mini-Chevy chrome	UPGRADE	$155.00
	Headers - T'coated	$310.00	
	Intake - carburetor - not required with 355 HP	$175.00	
	Carburetor - Holley 650	$325.00	
	Electric fuel pump in line	$74.00	
	Exhaust system w/mufflers aluminized	$450.00	
	Harmonic balancer - not required with 355 HP	$88.00	
	Radiator - Griffin aluminum 2 rows 1-1/4" tubes	$560.00	
	Radiator hoses	$60.00	
	Radiator cap	$20.00	
	Electric fan - Spal 16 inch & t'stat switch	$170.00	
	Spark plugs & wires	$75.00	

	Spark plug wire looms	$40.00	
	Automotive belts	$30.00	
	Distributor - not required with 355 HP	$165.00	
	Coil - not required with 355 HP	$40.00	
	Air cleaner - chrome	$40.00	
	Air cleaner - Billet	UPGRADE	$70.00
	Valve covers & breathers (2) - Billet	UPGRADE	$160.00
	Throttle cable, kickdown, bracket & spring - Lokar	$109.00	
	Water neck	$30.00	
	Engine & transmission dipsticks - Lokar	$103.00	
	Oil, transmission fluid, anti-freeze	$46.00	
	Battery, cables, eyes & cut off switch	$225.00	
	Wiring harness - 18 circuit	UPGRADE	$325.00
	TOTAL	**$5,219.00**	
TRANS			
	Type 350 w/torque converter	$1,200.00	
	Type 700R w/torque converter & electrical	UPGRADE	$600.00
	Shifter - Lokar - 12 inch - 350/700R w/boot	$205.00	
	Transmission cooler & hoses	$55.00	
	Flex plate & bolts - not required with 355 HP	$65.00	
	Transmission dust cover 350/700R	$65.00	
	TOTAL	**$1,590.00**	
ACCES			
	Gauges Dakota Digital w/bezel	UPGRADE	$550.00
	Gauges - VDO w/bezel	UPGRADE	$345.00
	Steering column - ididit paintable tilt & drop & floor mount	$376.00	
	Steering column - Mullins drop & flr mnt	UPGRADE	$141.00
	Steering joints With rod - 3 joints, heim & rod	$247.00	
	Steering wheel - LeCarra - Mark 9	$125.00	
	Steering wheel adaptor - polished	$69.00	
	7 channel remote w/actuators - Balls	UPGRADE	$280.00
	Door handles - nostalgia inside or door latch knobs	$30.00	
	Wheels & lug nuts - American polished torque thrusters	$750.00	
	Tires - radials mounted	$300.00	
	License plate frame - Billet light	UPGRADE	$50.00
	Third brake light LED - Gearhead	UPGRADE	$95.00

	Insulation - Koolmat & bubble foil	UPGRADE	$350.00
	Outside Mirrors - Billet	UPGRADE	$120.00
	Rear view mirror - Billet	$53.00	
	Heat & air conditioning unit - Vintage Air - Gen II Compact	UPGRADE	$405.00
	Compressor - plain - Sanden	UPGRADE	$200.00
	Compressor - chrome - Sanden	UPGRADE	$280.00
	Condenser - Vintage Air	UPGRADE	$139.00
	Trinary Switch - Vintage Air	UPGRADE	$51.00
	Hose kit & dryer - black - Vintage Air	UPGRADE	$100.00
	Hose kit & dryer - chrome - Vintage Air	UPGRADE	$169.00
	Gas,& brake pedal - Lokar	$112.00	
	Switch kit - ignition, light,	$50.00	
	TOTAL	**$2,112.00**	
PAINT			
	Paint engine, transmission	UPGRADE	$100.00
	Grind, smooth, paint - engine, transmission	UPGRADE	$1,200.00
	Grind smooth frame, rear end housing - paint	UPGRADE	$1,400.00
	All suspension pieces, MC, brake pedal arm, etc. - powder coat	UPGRADE	$400.00
	Paint body, fenders, hood, doors, underneath, etc.	UPGRADE	$6,500.00
	Paint price depends on color(s) or graphic(s)		
	TOTAL	**$**	
INTERIOR			
	Interior cloth (herculon), Glide seats or Tea's Design	UPGRADE	$5,500.00
	Leather or any customized interior would be subject to price.		
	Convertible top bid from upholster only.		
	TOTAL	**$**	
	LABOR TOTAL	**$5,500.00**	
	GRAND TOTAL	**$31,923.00**	

This is an estimate of the above written parts and labor. Parts prices are subject to invoice. Any additions or changes to this estimate will be subject to additional charges for parts and labor.

Chapter 3

Metal and Fiberglass Bodies

There are two ways to go when it comes to hot rod car bodies — metal or fiberglass. The greatest advantage of a steel car is that the body and the frame were made for each other and already fit. Providing that you don't make radical changes, you should feel comfortable that the body will set on the frame nicely. The exact opposite is true for fiberglass bodies. It is very unusual for a fiberglass body to mate to the chassis with no modifications. We will share some tips to make this chore easier if you end up with a fiberglass body, so don't panic if you bought a body already without planning this out.

Although metal-bodied cars are traditional and preferred by most professionals, there are times where fiberglass makes sense. Metal bodies usually have the advantage when it comes to spare parts because they are complete cars. They already have all of the little screws, brackets and hinges that are necessary to build the car. Fiberglass bodies rarely come as kits that include everything you need to assemble the car.

Overall, most professionals prefer metal-bodied cars because they have the tools to work with them, there is a wider variety of body styles to choose from and they have already acquired metal working skills. However, metal body modifications and rust repair can be difficult in a hobby environment. Expensive sandblasting, welding, cutting and grinding tools are needed in metal

(courtesy of Gibbon Fiberglass Reproductions)

There is a big difference between a completed car and the fiberglass body provided. Where will all the lights, trim, wiring harness, glass, etc., come from? Be sure to ask before you buy.

Rust holes in the floor are common. By themselves, they can be fixed for a reasonable price, but they usually indicate there is more hidden rust to be found.

work. It can be extremely time consuming as well. I recall several occasions where I stepped back from a major rust repair, scratched my head and asked "Was this really worth it? Why did I bother with this one again?" Remember that time is money in this hobby. It is very rare to find a metal car body that is less work than a fiberglass one. We'll discuss how to inspect a metal car, but most of the good metal donor cars have all been purchased by now.

Certainly, any "non-Ford" street rodders will be using metal bodies as donor cars. Ford is, and most likely will always be, the most popular street rod to build, so there is a wide selection of choices in fiberglass for early Ford. This is not the case for most anything else.

THE BIG DECISION

The choice of the car itself has probably led to more failed restoration and rod attempts than any other. Picking a donor car to start with is an important step in the plan. It is very tempting to draw out a car on a napkin, get really excited and go buy the first thing you see so you can get started as soon as possible. The enthusiasm is wonderful, but consider the entire road to automotive success to be peppered with land mines.

By the time we go car hunting, we should have a custom style laid out with some rough sketches of what the finished product should look like. We should know the year or years that are acceptable to use, what kind of chassis to use and what modifications will be made.

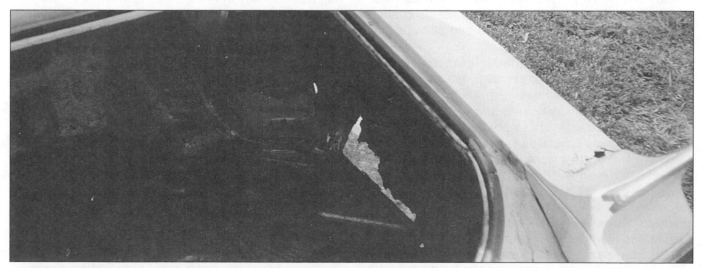

The light-colored area inside this trunk is actually a large hole. When inspecting a metal body, carefully study the firewall, floor and trunk for any holes larger than 1/4 inch.

This frame has rusted all the way through. Such cars should be avoided and considered a total loss. You could easily rack up $20,000 in rust repair expenses on a car like this.

We also should have a rough idea what the interior and exterior will look like, including what exterior trim will be used. Knowing whether or not we need all the trim moldings and chrome bumpers is important before we select the donor vehicle.

Above all we should have a budget, not just for the finished project, but it should be broken out to include what we are going to spend for a donor vehicle.

SHOPPING TIPS

Most of a street rod or custom car is painted, chromed, removed or modified, so we don't necessarily need a mint-condition original for the donor. As a matter of fact, a mint-condition vehicle is not preferred. You will pay top dollar for one and only dismantle or destroy most of it anyway. What we really need to do is only pay for the critical parts we need.

For example, does the car even need to have an engine? Most people use new power plants in their custom cars. Most people also build custom interiors, so the interior doesn't need to be nice. Some custom builders will design cars that don't need all the sheet metal.

Every builder will have a different plan, so I cannot take you through every specific step, but take a close look at the metal you need. Especially, look at the inside of the trunk, wheel wells and under the rocker panels or step boards. These areas are notorious for rust. Are there any special parts missing? For example, if you are looking at a convertible as a donor, does it have the top mechanism, top switch and rear seat? These parts are special to all convertibles and are very difficult to find. If we are using the chrome, it not only needs to be there, but all the steel parts should be straight and the pot metal parts should be void of pits. Both of these problems can force a builder to purchase new parts later down the road. Don't be hesitant to take a magnet with you. Areas with no magnetic pull either

have body filler or lead in them, which usually indicates a problem or older patchwork.

I recommend getting somewhat picky here. Builders looking at early model street rods have good fiberglass bodies and new frames to fall back on. Custom builders looking at 1940-'60s model custom cars have newer metal and thousands of good cars still on the roads. If the rust holes are larger than 1/4 inch in diameter or the vehicle has been wrecked in any way, pass. There are other choices out there.

The Internet is a wonderful tool. It can save so much time, but I'm horrified every time I hear of people putting deposits down or buying cars without even seeing them. Never buy sight unseen. Take the time to see the car and inspect it with your own eyes. Photographs save time initially, but they only tell a part of the story.

FIBERGLASS KITS

Fiberglass bodies and kits can lead to a whole new nightmare. Many of the kits do not fit together well and require major re-engineering to complete. The details here can kill you.

I recommend a few steps to protect yourself. First, I would not purchase a fiberglass kit unless you have a recommendation from a friend or club member. Let somebody else be the guinea pig. If you meet someone who has built a kit from a specific manufacturer with good results and limited frustration, then by all means use that vendor. I so strongly suggest using that vendor, that I would even alter my plan, if necessary, to accommodate the new vendor's specs.

The second piece of advice is don't just buy a body, look for a whole kit. Someone who has thought the whole kit out has more than likely built his own product and refined it. You would be surprised how many vendors haven't even built their own product before.

Take special interest in the way the kit fits together. How did the manufacturer engineer the door, trunk and

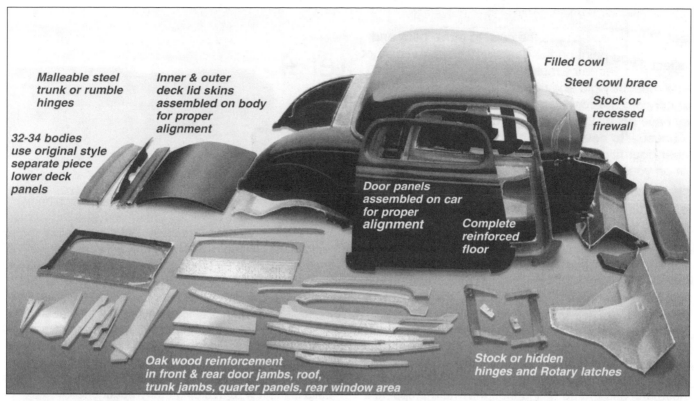

Malleable steel
trunk or rumble
hinges

Inner & outer
deck lid skins
assembled on body
for proper
alignment

Filled cowl

Steel cowl brace

Stock or
recessed
firewall

32-34 bodies
use original style
separate piece
lower deck
panels

Door panels
assembled on car
for proper
alignment

Complete
reinforced
floor

Oak wood reinforcement
in front & rear door jambs, roof,
trunk jambs, quarter panels, rear window area

Stock or hidden
hinges and Rotary latches

(courtesy of Gibbon Fiberglass Reproductions)

This manufacturer has put a lot of thought into the engineering of this kit. Note all the oak reinforcement and construction options.

hood hinges? I have seen some kits where the hinges screw right into the fiberglass using home door hinges and wood screws! Of course, this is more than likely found on the lowest-priced kits, so keep in mind that you do get what you pay for. Remember, most hinges are hard steel and fiberglass is fairly soft. The two don't go together well and creative engineering is required to solve this problem.

When you are looking for vendors, look for one that offers a kit where the doors, trunk and hood come pre-mounted. Most of the higher-quality vendors offer this service for about $1,000 more, and it can be worth every cent. Do not be fooled into thinking this is an easy task. I would guess that if a vendor doesn't offer this service, it is a red flag that something is wrong with the kit itself.

Take a close look at how the body is finished. This may mean you have to take a trip to the factory to see the manufacturing process. Ask people who have built the kit questions concerning the amount of time that was needed to get the body straight before painting. Fiberglass bodies have a reputation for being very wavy. The more questions you ask, the better. And remember, you pay for a kit up front and have very few return options. Let the buyer beware when it comes to fiberglass.

Chapter 4

Chassis

The most common mistake in street rodding starts out something like this: You know from your budgeting that you will have about $7,000 in the chassis, the same in the engine and transmission, another $10,000 in the fiberglass body kit and another $10,000 in miscellaneous costs like interior and paint. What most people do is spread the cost out over the duration of the project.

For example, they buy the frame this month and later buy some suspension parts and slowly put the chassis together over time. They paint the finished chassis and move on to the engine. Maybe a year goes by before they purchase the body and then they start prepping it for paint. They have a gorgeous chassis costing 15 grand or more and a newly painted body ready to go.

Then one day they invite their friends over to watch and help lower the body to the chassis. It is on this day that all the problems arise. First the firewall hits the engine and scuffs up the paint. Then the rear tires either stick out too far from fenders or rub on the inner fender wells. Then the brake and gas pedals don't line up. A few dozen choice words are said and eventually the blame goes to the kit manufacturer for providing a crummy kit. Some $25,000-plus are wasted and the project comes to a screeching halt — often for good.

Once again, this is the direct result of poor planning. Buying the car piece by piece and building it over time can work, but it usually ends up being more expensive. The big lesson here: *Always perform a rough build before any painting or final assembly takes place.* You need the complete chassis, wheels, tires, engine, transmission and all the major body parts. This makes up almost 2/3 of the total price of the car so buying all of this at once needs to be part of your plan. If this is impossible, then just keep in mind that you will be storing the parts for a while before any real work can begin, and this takes quite a bit of discipline. The rough build is the key to avoiding many headaches.

WELDING CHOICES

Michael Young, owner of Street Rods by Michael in Shelbyville, Tennessee, knows how to do things right. He has been building rods for more than 30 years.

So let's see how Young does it.

The basic frame is built first and Young starts with a frame rail kit from American Stamping. The rail kit comes with the boxing plates and outer frame rails. Even though you can buy pre-manufactured cross members, Young prefers to build these himself using tubular steel. Over years he has found these cross

Many builders feel the chassis is one of the most enjoyable parts of the build process. With the body off the car, the mechanics are easy to see and enjoy.

(courtesy of Street Rods by Michael)

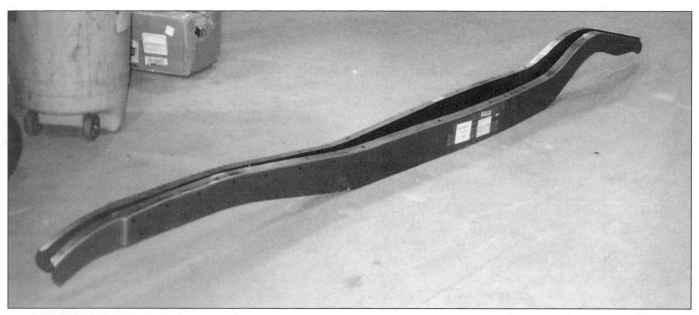

(courtesy of Street Rods by Michael)

The chassis starts with the frame rails. Michael Young prefers non-boxed or C channel frame rails because they have a smooth, original appearance. He then welds the inner plate himself to get the finished, full-boxed frame rail.

members increase strength while leaving more room for exhaust components later on.

The frame rails are first placed in a jig and bolted in at the spreader bar hole locations. In order to get a clean, smooth look, the wrinkled areas caused by the stamping process are hammered out with a dolly. The inner frame rails are cut to fit and tack welded in place. He uses both MIG and TIG welding during the construction of his frames. Most people are using MIG welders now, mainly to reduce equipment costs. There are differing opinions on which of the two are the strongest welds, but both TIG and MIG welding can provide plenty of strength provided the proper technique is used.

In order for a MIG welder to achieve its full strength, there needs to be about a 1/16-inch gap between the two welding surfaces. This allows the MIG welding wire to melt both surfaces properly. TIG welding proves useful in areas where there is no gap at all because it has the ability to melt deeper into the steel. In general, Young uses a MIG weld to complete the boxed frame rails and a TIG welder to assemble and install the tubular cross members.

SUSPENSION DECISIONS

After the frame rails are centered in the jig and measurements are taken, the center cross member is

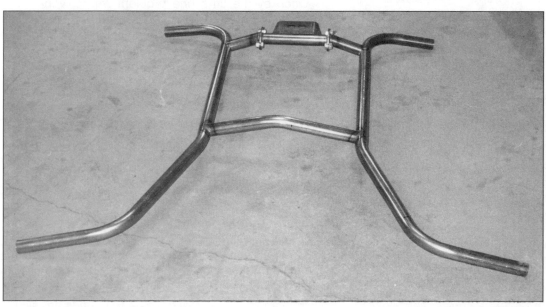

Young builds the center cross member himself using tubular steel. The transmission mount bolts on to allow easy transmission removal later.

(courtesy of Street Rods by Michael)

(courtesy of Street Rods by Michael)

John Young, Michael's son, prepares to lay a TIG weld on this rear cross member. TIG welds are perfect for tubular steel construction.

(courtesy of Street Rods by Michael)

This close-up of the center cross member shows nice, even heat distribution around the welds. The bracket on the left is used to hold the front portion of a four-bar rear suspension.

installed. The rear cross member is nothing more than a tube or C-channel piece of steel and it, too, is welded into place. The front cross member is next and it is at this point where we have some choices. The front cross member can change depending on what type of suspension will be used.

When hot rods were first built in the 1930s and 40s, there weren't too many suspension options. Most people focused on reducing weight and horsepower. As better suspensions were introduced in new cars, rodders sought ways to incorporate these changes into the older cars. The easiest way to accomplish this was to replace the rear axle assembly and weld in the front cross member of a Mustang II or Pinto.

Most subframe replacements were done on post-1934 cars, however, and several problems were eventually discovered. First, when the original frame stubs were removed, all of the mounting locations for sheet metal and radiator support were lost. New ones had to be measured and drilled. Also, it was uncommon that wide tires would set correctly and this limited the choice of wheel rims rodders could use. Many of the steering boxes would mount close to, or interfere with, the headers. The brakes at the rear of the car were also affected because many of the donor brakes used the emergency brake to constantly reseat the rear pads. Many rodders left the emergency brake off because it can be difficult to set up and within a month were riding on the front pads only and wondering why.

Often by the time one problem was solved a new technology would come out and create a whole new set of problems. Fortunately, the technology has stabilized and the modifications are getting easier to handle. There are two broad styles of front suspension used today: The straight axle and the independent front suspension (IFS).

STRAIGHT AXLES

The straight axle is most commonly found on lighter cars from 1928-'34. A straight axle is essentially what was used on most of the older cars originally, but several common modifications have been made to improve performance. The split wishbone was perhaps the first. A split wishbone improves handling by moving the pivot point towards the outside of the frame and widening the stance.

Much of hot rodding and custom work is "looks," so you see many suspension innovations based on this. Hairpin and four-bar straight axle front ends are similar

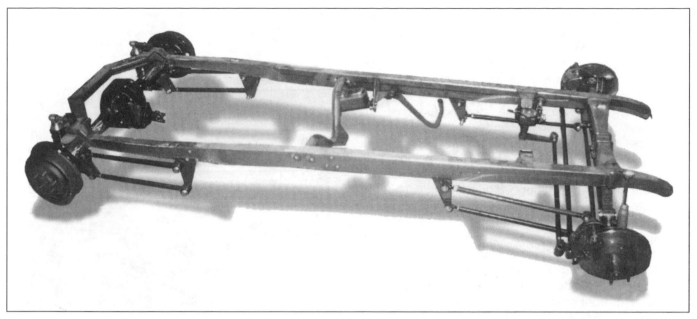

(courtesy of Gibbon Fiberglass Reproductions)

This is an example of a four-bar front and rear suspension that is versatile enough for most of the smaller, early-1930s street rods.

and evolved from this need. This technology uses slender tubular bars to secure the spindle in place. A hairpin uses three contact points to the frame and the four-bar uses four contacts. The four-bar setup is the most commonly used in early styled hot rods today. Four-bar suspension is almost always found on high boy or fenderless cars. It has a clean, elegant look to it.

The "pinched" front end is another type of straight axle found on fenderless cars. This is similar to a four-bar setup but is modified so the frame rails narrow and

tuck in behind the radiator for a clean, sleek look. Pinched front ends also use coil overs in the front instead of transverse springs and shocks. A good source for straight axle components is Pete and Jake's Hot Rod Parts.

As previously noted, straight axles are normally used on lighter cars. They historically had poor handling and "bump steer" problems, but much of this has been eliminated. The steering problems were mainly caused by using a Mustang steering box, which had a

Here is a good shot of a pinched front end. Notice that the frame rails are hidden behind the radiator. The detail on the front of the car is the most appreciated as some of it can be seen with the hood up and most people will want to look inside your hood. Try to place your contrast of color with aluminum and chrome in the front if the budget allows.

(courtesy of Street Rods by Michael)

long drag link that went from the pitman arm to the driver's side front spindle. The driver would feel the steering wheel jump or shake when the wheels hit a pothole or bump in the road. This is called bump steer. Keep in mind that early rods had no front sway bars either, which didn't help.

The newer Chevrolet Vega steering box uses a cross steer system, which is shorter and pushes on the passenger side spindle instead of the driver's side. This steering keeps the suspension in line over bumps. This change has greatly improved bump steer on straight axle front ends. An experienced or professional hot rod and frame builder should be used in mounting both suspension and steering components. Steering components must have parallel symmetry to both the ground, the frame and themselves in order to eliminate bump steer and make the car safe to drive. This is somewhat complicated. Some people have sought out independent front suspension as a means to eliminate bump steer — which leads us to the other front suspension, IFS.

INDEPENDENT FRONT SUSPENSION (IFS)

One of the first IFS donor cars was the Corvair. However, when the Mustang II was introduced in the '70s, it quickly became the new standard in IFS for custom cars and now all independent front suspension is called Mustang II suspension — whether the parts come from the car or not. A wide variety of IFS kits are available today; the least expensive of which uses the entire set of parts out of an original Mustang II and then replaces the worn parts like brake pads.

This solution does have some problems. Most of these problems are the same that you get with grafting in the entire front frame portion of vehicles. IFS is larger than the original straight axle, so stock Mustang parts rub the inside fenders of many models. It is also not used much on fenderless cars like high boys for similar reasons. IFS is bulky and odd-looking on high boys, but this is somewhat irrelevant if you are building a custom car with fenders.

Stock Mustang IFS parts also can lead to the same wider-than-original wheel track and limit your options in wheel selection. Several companies recognized this and began designing custom cross members with tubular 'A' arms to fit most any car and eliminate the stock problems. One of the leaders in this field is Fat Man Fabrications. They offer almost any IFS part you'll need.

IFS generally handles better than the straight axle, but it too, has a few drawbacks. To eliminate bump steer, you need to have all of the steering components lined up as precisely as the straight axle, so I also recommend you have a professional install your IFS components. Many a rodder has bought an IFS kit, installed it themselves and immediately noticed the same bump steer or worse.

Other than the bulky look on fenderless cars and the precision needed in the installation, IFS really has no

(courtesy of Street Rods by Michael)

One look at a front cross member used for an independent front suspension.

other cons. It is actually preferred in all of the larger custom cars starting with '35 and up. Kits can be located to help you install IFS all the way up through the '60s, so it can be utilized on almost any custom project. Another advantage to independent front suspension is that it uses a rack steering box, which will give you a modern, precision feel to your handling on the road. One criticism of IFS is the cost. A complete IFS kit with new parts runs between $2,000 and $2,500. Keep in mind that straight axles can be found in the $1,700 range, but you need to factor in the cost of a steering box and mount. When this is calculated, the IFS is only $100 more or so. They end up being real close.

REAR SUSPENSION CHOICES

The rear suspension also has choices. On almost any car we work on, we'll find leaf spring suspension used at the rear of the car. Most people still prefer leaf springs on the heavier 1935-and-later models simply because leaf springs handle the heavier weights well.

Remember that leaf springs attach to a moving shackle at the rear of the frame. This is done to allow the springs to flex on severe bumps. When leaf springs flex, they end up pushing the rear axle toward the rear of the car. With the exception of Indiana Jones, few of us have been able to see this happen, you need to figure in about an inch and a half of play front and back. This could be significant if you are designing custom wheel wells. There needs to be some space between the rear tire and the body of the car.

Leaf springs use traditional shocks and there are some limitations as to how you adjust leaf springs for ride height. The primary reason why you don't see rear leaf springs often in 1934-and-earlier is that the springs end up being so short that you get a very stiff, uncomfortable ride.

(courtesy of Street Rods by Michael)

A finished frame without suspension parts installed.

Just like the four-bar setup on the front of these 1930s models, you typically see four-bar setups in the rear. Unlike the front end, however, there are several variations of four-bar set ups in the rear.

The traditional four-bar runs the suspension rods parallel to the frame and uses a panhard bar to reduce lateral movement of the axle. Even with the use of a panhard bar, a slight side-to-side movement can be felt in more extreme cornering, which has prompted a modification of this setup to what is called a "triangular" four-bar setup. The top bars on this setup are angled in, which eliminates the need for a panhard bar. Once the panhard bar is removed from the equation, the exhaust is much easier to install.

For the triangular four-bar setup, the axle housing must be centered under the car. You would be surprised to find out how many cars have a drive shaft that runs at an angle under the car. Triangular four-bar set-ups must have a centered housing to work properly.

The ladder-bar setup is much like a hairpin setup for the rear. The bars are longer and reinforced, which helps torque the wheels down to the ground. A ladder bar is recommended if you are building a high-horsepower engine, but otherwise they are difficult to run exhaust through.

Another type of suspension is the "pro street" setup. Pro street cars are like any other hot rod except they use massive rear tires normally found on dragsters. Pro street bodies require extensive floor and wheel well modification to accommodate the extra-wide tires. This system is an extra-narrow four-bar setup and uses a diagonal link instead of the standard panhard bar to stabilize the rear end. All four use coil overs instead of the traditional spring and shock.

Coil overs are nice because they are easily adjustable for ride height. Just remember that they act as your shocks, too. Many rodders will try to use them to increase ride height to the point where the coil overs are almost fully extended. This is essentially riding on steel, so your first speed bump will probably knock your fillings loose. (Never take hot rodding advice from a dentist.)

(courtesy of Street Rods by Michael)

A good look at a triangular four-bar setup. Notice that the top bars are angled to give lateral support.

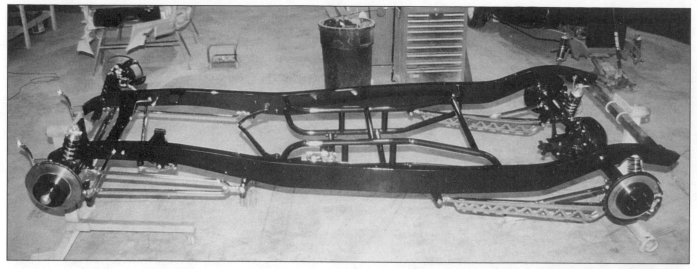

(courtesy of Gibbon Fiberglass Reproductions)

This is a good view of a ladder-bar suspension in the rear. Ladder bars are good for performance situations like drag racing, but are not as useful in common street cruising because of their low profile.

SELECTING A REAR END

With the frame and suspension completed, we now need a rear end and differential. How do we know how to get a rear end and axles that are the correct width so our tires do not touch the body or stick out too far? This question needs to be asked on every street rod project.

It is at this point that a rough build of the car becomes necessary. We need to mount the body to the frame first. Line the body up so that it is straight down the axis of the frame and centered from left to right. The body needs to be placed from front to back so that the rear wheel housing is centered above the rear axle housing location.

The body, whether it is steel or fiberglass, will have several body-mount locations so the floor can bolt to the frame. Cars from the late 1940s and later use rubber insulators between the frame and body. These can be located from Steele Rubber Co. Hot rodders usually use the stock frame in those years, so all you need to do is replace the rubber mounts and you are finished.

If you are using a fiberglass body, most kit manufacturers request that you send the chassis to them so they can custom manufacture the floor section to fit your chassis. This is necessary in the sense that every chassis is different and if you do not utilize this step, you may need some pretty radical shimming to get your doors to line up properly.

Most kits use a cloth-like mesh material as the body mount and this can be provided by the kit manufacturer. Some frames have tabs or ears that come off the frame for

Coil overs act as both the shock and spring. They are also adjustable for proper ride height. Do not overextend the adjustment on your coil overs as you will lose both your shock absorber and suspension effect.

(courtesy of Street Rods by Michael)

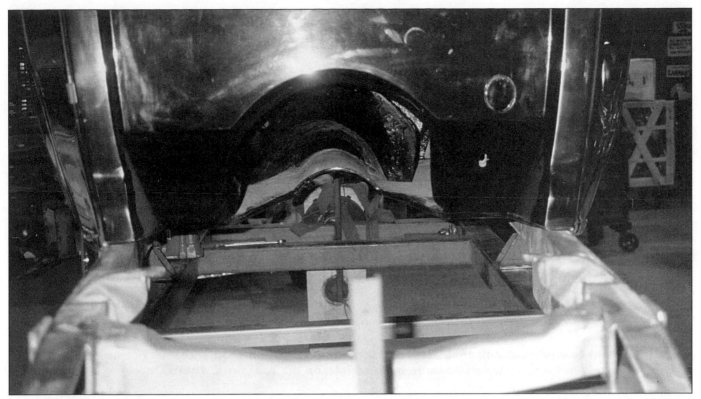

(courtesy of Street Rods by Michael)

When using fiberglass bodies, it is recommended that you send the chassis to the body manufacturer. They will custom manufacture a floor to your chassis so the body mounts line up and the doors fit properly.

the mounts and some frames have threaded holes right down into the frame. All mounts need to be checked at this point to see if they line up between the frame and floor.

(courtesy of Street Rods by Michael)

When you lower the body to the frame, there should be enough room for the drive shaft and exhaust system. Be sure to check your body mounts to see if they line up to the mounts on the frame. If they do not, mark the appropriate changes so the mounts can be moved.

CHECKING THE FIT

To get the proper rear-end width, mount the finished tires to the rims and roll them into their final location at the rear of the car. If you are not building a high boy, then you will need to mount the fenders as well. You can use jacks and jack stands to position the frame and body over the tires so that they do not touch any portion of the body and they have sufficient ride clearance up and down. Custom steel-bodied cars with wider-than-stock tires usually need a floor and inner wheel well modification to allow for the larger tires. Your measurements and modifications could be made at this point.

The most important measurement you will need for the proper rear-end width is the distance between the two mounting surfaces on the wheel rims. The mounting surface of the rim is the area that physically touches the disc rotor or drum. With the wheels in place, take a measurement across the width of the car from the inside mounting surface of one wheel across to the other. You should be able to contact any rear end shop at this point and give them this measurement and they will be able to provide you the proper rear end with axles included. When the rear end arrives, go ahead and install the rear end, coil overs, brakes and tires and double check that your measurements were indeed accurate.

ENGINE CONSIDERATIONS

With the rear end and body mounts finished, it's time to check the location of the engine, transmission and

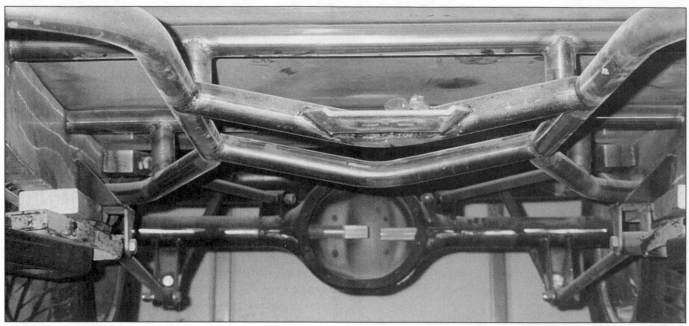

(courtesy of Street Rods by Michael)

It's important to double check that the rear tire placement is centered and does not touch the body. The axles may not line up because there is no weight on the rear tires. That's OK.

brake master cylinder mounts. An engine and transmission assembly are needed first.

Now there are dozens of books that teach you how to build engines, so I believe it is redundant to cover that here, but what I want to caution you about is practicality and budgeting. You can drop 15 grand in an engine real fast, so what is the final goal here? Are we street cruising or racing? Do you need an 800-hp engine to move down the street? Please budget your engine line item by line item and research how much power and chrome you will need or be able to afford.

Flathead engines are very popular as they bring back some of the nostalgia of the early years. This engine, with the blower setup, ran about $12,000.

(courtesy of Street Rods by Michael)

This is a common example of a $15,000 engine. Even the casting on the engine block has been ground smooth so the paint slicks out like the outside of the car.

(courtesy of Street Rods by Michael)

Go back to the Web and research what engines cost and a good place to start is the pricing sheets on Michael Young's site. You can get a nice engine for $5,000. It won't be a show engine, but you can have the same amount of fun with it as the expensive ones. Let's go back to our pricing sheet and look at the example engine.

(courtesy of Street Rods by Michael)

The engine/transmission assembly is lowered to mark the locations for the engine mounts. The engine should be placed about 1 inch forward of the firewall.

ENGINE

Crate engine - SBC 230 HP		$1,700
Crate engine - SBC 330 HP	UPGRADE	$1,000
Crate engine - SBC 355 HP	UPGRADE	$2,000
Brackets - Alan Grove alternator		$70
Brackets - Billet Specialties polished A/C/Alt.	UPGRADE	$130
Pulleys - Chevrolet stock steel pulleys		$80
Pulleys - Billet Specialties V-belt polished	UPGRADE	$60
Alternator - 100 amp – chrome		$124
Water pump - plain SW		$35
Water pump - Tuff-Stuff chrome SW	UPGRADE	$60
Starter – plain		$75
Starter - PowerMaster mini-Chevy chrome	UPGRADE	$155
Headers - T'coated		$310
Intake - carburetor - not required with 355 HP		$175
Carburetor - Holley 650		$325
Fuel pump, plate, pin, rod		$110
Exhaust system w/mufflers aluminized		$450
Harmonic balancer - not required with 355 HP		$88
Radiator - Griffin aluminum 2 rows 1-1/4" tubes		$610
Radiator hoses		$60
Radiator cap		$20
Electric fan - Spal 16 inch & t'stat switch		$170
Spark plugs & wires		$74
Spark plug wire looms		$25
Automotive belts		$30
Distributor - not required with 355 HP		$165
Coil - not required with 355 HP		$40
Air cleaner – chrome		$50
Air cleaner - Billet polished ball milled	UPGRADE	$70
Valve covers & breathers (2) – Billet	UPGRADE	$160
Throttle cable, kickdown, bracket & spring		$109
Water neck		$30
Engine & transmission dipsticks		$103
Oil, transmission fluid, anti-freeze		$46
Battery, cables, eyes & cut off switch		$225
Wiring harness - 18 circuit	UPGRADE	$325
Basic Total		**$5,299**

Men of all ages love engines. Here, Bill Kyzer's grandson, Cody, helps stabilize the engine as Michael Young lowers it to the frame.

(courtesy of Street Rods by Michael)

The mounts are welded in place when the engine is removed.

(courtesy of Street Rods by Michael)

As you can see, this basic, but complete, hot rod engine will cost us just over $5,000. Don't forget that hot rods are small and don't have much weight to them anyway, so the large engines can end up being over

kill. As we go up in price, we are gaining horsepower and chrome. A common engine in the $15,000 range would have extras like these:

502 big block with aluminum heads	$6,955
Block castings ground smooth and painted	$1,000
Aluminum heads polished	$400
Chrome tune port injection, wire harness and sensors	$3,895
Chrome alternator and A/C brackets	$295
Coated headers	$425
Chrome pulleys	$700
Chrome power steering pump and reservoir	$430
Chrome A/C compressor	$425
Chrome water pump	$105
Chrome alternator	$155
Chrome valve covers	$250
Performance cam	$185

(courtesy of Street Rods by Michael)

The engine should be reinstalled to check the location of the mounts. Carburetors need to be level to work properly. Adjust your transmission mount location so that the engine becomes level to the ground.

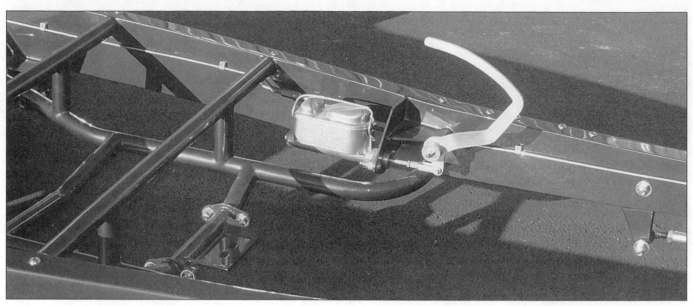

(courtesy of Street Rods by Michael)

It's important not to overlook the placement of items such as the master cylinder and pedal assemblies.

Oh, and don't forget stainless steel gas tanks run between $500 and $800. Keep in mind that the gas tanks don't normally come with sending units. The sending units come with your gauge set.

As you can see, it racks up real fast. Set a budget and stick to it. You're not going to have bragging rights over every car you see. There are some very deep pockets in this hobby, and the point of all this is to have fun.

I would not paint the engine at this point, but it's not the end of the world if it has already been done. Using the engine hoist, lower the engine/transmission assembly to the chassis so that it rests in its final position. I recommend having all of the suspension and tires

(courtesy of Street Rods by Michael)

The finished chassis with suspension. This has already had all measurements done for rear end width, engine/transmission mounts, body mounts and brake/gas peddles. Some builders will prime and paint the chassis as one piece to save time. I recommend painting the components separately.

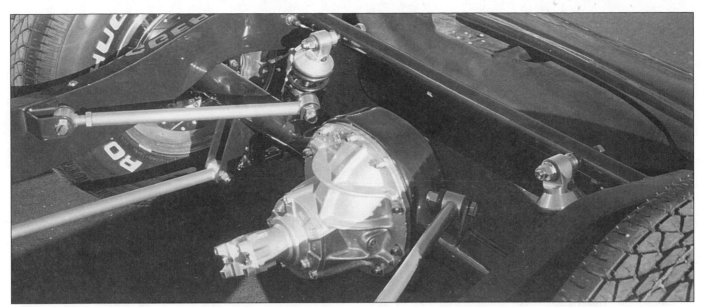

(courtesy of Street Rods by Michael)

Most of the detail seen here is necessary for show cars, but not for cruising street rods. If your plan starts to go over budget, cut out the chrome on the chassis as it is the least appreciated.

mounted at this time. The distributor needs to be installed. Bring the engine back so that the distributor rests about 1 inch off of the firewall.

If your car has larger rear tires, you may need to compensate for the rake by lowering or raising the transmission. This is required if your engine has a carburetor, but only needed on fuel-injected engines if you like the "look" of an engine that is parallel to the ground.

With the engine in its final location, move your engine mounts into position and mark their locations on the frame. One last thing to keep in mind is some engines have large air filters or blowers that will stick out above the hood. If you are building such a car, the hood will need to be mounted first and the engine raised up to its final location above the hood before the leveling process can begin. I would tack weld the engine mounts into position before addressing the transmission mount.

Once the engine mounts are in place, lower the engine assembly into position again. Mount the engine and start taking the weight off of the hoist. You can use a padded floor jack under the transmission to control its weight and elevation. Use the floor jack to get the proper engine elevation so that it is parallel to the ground and mark the position for the transmission mount. If the body is so low to the ground that it interferes with the work, you could move on to making your brake and gas pedal measurements and then lift the body out of the way to work on the transmission mount. It is recommended that you use a transmission mount that bolts to the frame or center cross member to allow for easy transmission removal in the future.

OTHER DETAILS

The last critical measurements involve the gas and brake pedals. Every pedal kit mounts differently —

some to the frame and others to the body itself. Either way a master cylinder or booster is almost always found on the frame just outside the pedal location.

All measurements and appropriate brackets need to be welded into place before any painting is done to the frame. Also, will you be using an electric fan to cool the radiator or a traditional engine-mounted one? Most rodders are having better luck with electric as they cool better in traffic and at lower speeds. It is a good idea to test mount the radiator and fan before painting as well. Any work, like brake lines or gas lines, that requires drilling on the frame should be done at this time.

Even when the chassis is essentially finished, you're probably still not at a point where you can paint the frame. Keep in mind that the body will be lowered to the frame for paint and body work so you are asking for all kinds of over spray-problems if you finish the chassis at this stage. It is a good idea to get your chassis in a coat of epoxy primer for rust protection, however. Please refer to the paint and body sections to learn proper metal preparation and the differences between paint and powder coating. If you go with powder coating, you should not prime any of the parts for any reason.

We will cover brakes in the next chapter, but keep in mind that final assembly should be fun. This is where all the hard work pays off and you get to see the fruit of your labor. Remember that you cannot easily see the chassis once the car is completed, so the expense of chrome-plated parts and bolts is often not fully appreciated later on. Chrome is necessary on show cars, but this would be the first place to cut if it looks like you are going over budget.

Chapter 5

Brakes

My first shop was run out of an airplane hanger and it never ceased to amaze me that people who knew little about airplanes and who never worked on one before would build kit airplanes and attempt to fly them. At least if you make a mistake with your car engine, you can usually pull over and call a tow truck. You don't have that luxury in the air and I feel brakes are just as serious.

For those who have never built a car before, you should enlist the help of a professional when it comes to most brake work. This is not the place to learn from your mistakes. One of the most challenging aspects of custom brakes is that everyone is doing something different. In other words, there is more than one way to skin a cat. This chapter gives you the overall picture, but others may have a slightly different view. You'll have to roll with the information as it is presented and weigh all the opinions.

It's important to treat the brakes as a singular system and not just a grouping of parts. This means that the cylinder, calipers, lines and master cylinder match each other. A common mistake that rodders make is

buying mismatched parts. Consult your brake parts supplier or builder and make sure you are buying parts that work together.

The most frequent complaint I hear about brakes in custom cars is a hard brake pedal. This is when you have to press down hard on the pedal to get the vehicle to stop. The extreme case would be the feeling that you have to "stand" on the brakes to get them to engage. Another problem happens when you apply the brakes and your rear tires lock up quickly, causing the rear end to fish tail. Of course the worst problem would be a complete brake failure, when you press the pedal to the floor and nothing happens. There are usually simple explanations for these various problems.

In order to build a brake system properly, we need to first understand what all the individual parts do. The design of your braking system will change radically if you intend to race the car, but the vast majority of custom cars are built for cruising. This chapter will focus on conventional braking systems used in street rods and passenger cars.

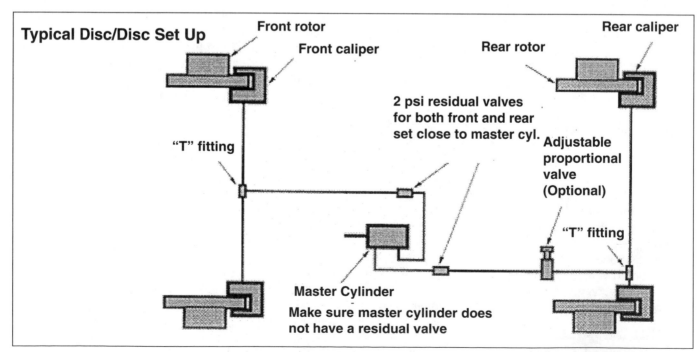

Typical Disc/Disc Set Up

Front rotor
Front caliper
Rear caliper
Rear rotor

2 psi residual valves for both front and rear set close to master cyl.

Adjustable proportional valve (Optional)

"T" fitting

"T" fitting

Master Cylinder

Make sure master cylinder does not have a residual valve

(courtesy of Engineered Components, Inc.)

This is a typical disc/disc setup. Notice that the 10-lb. residual valve goes to the rear brakes only and the 2-lb. valve is needed if your master cylinder is lower than the calipers.

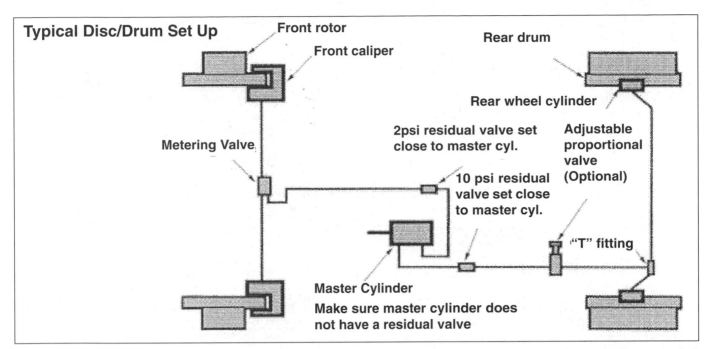

Typical Disc/Drum Set Up

Front rotor

Front caliper

Rear drum

Rear wheel cylinder

Metering Valve

2psi residual valve set close to master cyl.

Adjustable proportional valve (Optional)

10 psi residual valve set close to master cyl.

"T" fitting

Master Cylinder

Make sure master cylinder does not have a residual valve

(courtesy of Engineered Components, Inc.)

On a typical disc/drum setup, the front metering valve is replaced with a common "T" fitting and residual valves are only needed if the master cylinder is mounted lower than the calipers. The best example is found on cylinders mounted below the floor.

TYPES OF BRAKES

There are essentially two styles of brakes: disc and drum. The most common factory setup today uses both. You see discs in the front and drums in the back. If you remember back to your bicycle days, if you pressed the back brake only, you came to a slow stop. If you pressed the front only, you could flip over the handle bars. The best idea was to learn how to use both. Well, automotive brakes are similar in some ways.

The front brakes do most of the work. This is because the weight of the vehicle shifts to the front during the stop. To test this, watch the front end of your everyday driver dip down the next time you have to brake hard in traffic. If you were to pick up a disc, you would have your thumb on one side and your fingers on the other. You pick the disc up by squeezing it so that it doesn't slip out of your hand. This is how disc brakes work. The metal disc is called a rotor and your hand is the caliper. The caliper holds a brake pad on either side of the rotor and uses hydraulic pressure to squeeze the rotor to a stop. If this happens while the car is still moving, your tires lock up and you lose control. Anti-lock brake systems (ABS) have sensors

Note that this rotor is both vented and has extra holes for cooling.

(courtesy of Street Rods by Michael)

that detect this and use a computer to pulse the calipers on and off so they don't lock up. Drum brakes use pads that press outward on the inside of a metal drum. The friction slows the movement of the drum and brings the car to a stop.

If you are using drum-style brakes at the rear of the car, the brakes generally come with the donor rear end. So if you select a 1967-'74 Camaro rear end, then you will use those same drum brakes. Companies like Engineered Components Inc. can provide the rebuild kits for most rear ends you come across. If you are using a chassis builder, ask them which rear end and braking system will work best for your frame.

Early hot rods typically use a Ford 8- or 9-inch rear end. Cars up through the 1950s and '60s most likely will use the stock rear end and drum brakes and use a kit to replace the worn parts. Disc brakes are almost always used on the front and sometimes on the rear as well. None of these older cars that we are working with had disc brakes, so a completely new kit will be needed to accomplish this. Most of the front end suppliers mentioned previously also supply the appropriate brakes.

ROTORS

There are two basic types of discs or rotors. Solid rotors are commonly used on early hot rods and are the least expensive. A vented rotor is hollow with small vents in the center to help cool the rotor down during heavy braking. Both styles can have extra holes drilled throughout the surface of the rotor to assist with cooling as well. Solid rotors will not cool as well as vented ones, so they are not recommended for cars weighing more than 2,800 lbs. Most pre-1933 hot rods are close to 2,500 lbs. and are kind

of on the borderline for use with solid rotors. When in doubt, use vented rotors, as they do not cost much more. Cars past '35 are almost always more than 2,800 lbs., so you should consider vented rotors on just about every car past that. Remember that the larger the diameter of your rotors or drums, the less frequently the pad will be touching any one spot, which helps reduce heat.

CALIPERS

There are two types of calipers available: floating and non-floating. Floating calipers are the most common and are found on most OEM brakes. This caliper has one hydraulic piston that operates the pads on either side of the rotor. They are affordable and have several advantages. Should your rotor have a slight depression or imperfection on the surface, the caliper will ride over the area freely much like the arm of an old record player. Floating calipers are also easier to bleed and maintain. They are more likely to flex, so most manufacturers make them out of iron or steel.

Most racing applications use a non-floating caliper, which has a piston on either side of the rotor. They are less likely to flex so the lighter, stiffer, heat-resistant metals can be used. They are more difficult to use and maintain.

BRAKE LINES

Next comes the brake lines, which can be another source of total brake failure. Brake lines are either made out of stainless or milled steel. Stainless is mainly used for looks as it maintains its silver finish and doesn't oxidize, however, it is much more difficult to install. Normal steel brake lines use a standard flaring tool that puts a double flare at a 45-degree angle. This

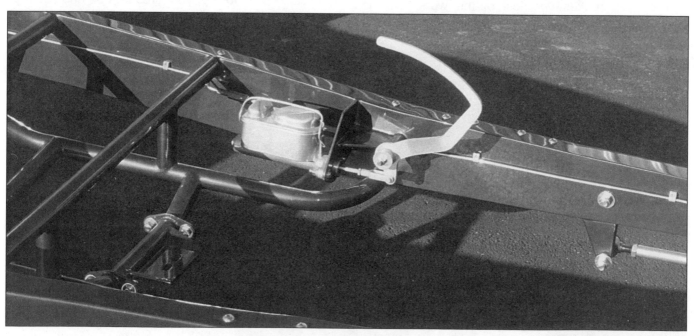

(courtesy of Street Rods by Michael)

This master cylinder is already mounted to the frame.

is what normal brake fittings use and if flared properly, they will not leak. Stainless steel is much harder, so if you try to use standard brake line tools, you will either split the end of the brake line or break the tool. Stainless is also much more difficult to bend.

If you choose stainless, you will need to use A/N (Army/Navy) fittings to prevent leaks. A/N fittings use a single flare at a 37-degree angle. There are special A/N fitting tools available for this. If you mix these two fittings up, your system will leak or fail. Most states also require a double flair on all brake lines, so if your brakes fail because of the wrong flair, you could find yourself personally liable for an accident. Most people use stainless only in show car applications.

The most common brake line diameter used is 3/16 inch, but there are exceptions. Some calipers or cylinders require more volume and may need larger, 1/4-inch lines. This is why it is important to view brakes as a complete system. Some parts require special items to work properly.

One word of caution: Never use compression fittings on your brake lines. They can blow out under high pressure, and will result in a total brake failure.

VALVES

Located in the lines are a series of valves. Many times you don't know about these valves, because so many OEM applications build the valves into the master or wheel cylinders. Ask your brake supplier if these valves are built in. Many of the valves have more than one name, but if you describe the function, you should be able to communicate with the brake supplier what your needs are.

The first valve is a metering or hold-off valve. This is used in a disc/drum setup only and sees to it that the rear brakes engage just slightly before or at the same time as the front discs. This valve is not usually used on disc/disc setups.

Another valve is a proportional valve. It is used in both disc/drum and disc/disc setups, but not typically used with hold-off valves. Proportional valves allow the rear brakes to come on first, but also create a slight pressure delay to the rear brakes so they do not come on at full force as soon as the pedal is applied. In other words, you want the rear brakes to come on first so the car doesn't swap ends, but you don't want them to come on so strong that the rear locks up.

Proportional valves are often confused with adjustable proportional valves, which work much like a water faucet. Adjustable valves allow you to restrict the flow of brake fluid to a set of brakes. Most street rodders use them to reduce the strength of the rear brakes, which is not what they were designed to do. Originally, adjustable proportional valves were used in racing. Racers use two of these valves to control fluid moving right and left and then run the valve up into the passenger compartment. This allows them to reduce or shut off the brakes of one whole side of the car, which is very useful in oval track racing.

Pro street cars have very large rear tires and these rodders found that the tires grabbed or locked up more because of their larger surface area. They began using these valves to cut off some of the fluid to the rear brakes to bring balance back to the system. After the valve started working well for the pro street crowd, many rodders put them in their systems. It is common to see these valves set to a zero or nonfunctioning setting, because they are just not needed in non-racing hot rod and custom cars.

The last type of valve is referred to as a residual valve. Residual valves are used to maintain pressure in the lines and are needed in two cases. On disc/drum setups, a 10 psi residual valve is needed for the rear drum brakes. The cup seals inside a drum wheel cylinder are designed to seal in one direction so if 10 lbs. of pressure are not applied at all times, the seal will leak air into the lines every time you release the brake pedal. Keep in mind that many master cylinders designed for drum brakes already have a 10-lb. residual valve in place, so you may not need to add one. Ask your parts supplier which type you have.

Disc brakes do not need a residual valve unless the master cylinder is physically located below the brake calipers. A good rule of thumb to follow is that if the master cylinder is located on the firewall like most cars after 1934, the cylinder is higher than the calipers. If the master cylinder is located on the frame below the floor, then it is lower than the calipers so every time you release the brake pedal, brake fluid will have a tendency to run downhill back to the master cylinder. A 2-psi residual valve is needed to prevent this. One exception is in pro street cars where the rear end is elevated radically and ends up being higher than the master cylinder no matter what.

Just remember that if you are driving and you need to pump the brakes several times to build up pressure, there may be a problem with the residual valves or you may need to add them to the system.

PEDAL RATIO

Ultimately, a hard brake pedal may be due to a problem between the master cylinder and brake pedal. To better understand how they work together it helps to understand what pedal ratio is and how it interacts with the diameter of the master brake cylinder.

Pedal ratio is a measurement of how much leverage, and therefore force, will be applied to the master cylinder. The longer the lever that the brake pedal is attached to, the greater the force. So why aren't pedal arms 2 feet long? Well, they would stick way up into the passenger compartment, so there is a balance between length and practicality. High pedal ratios usually mean that you have to lift your foot up in the air off of the gas to apply brakes, and that is not user friendly.

One of the reasons for hard brake pedal is that the pedal ratio is too low, meaning the length of the pedal

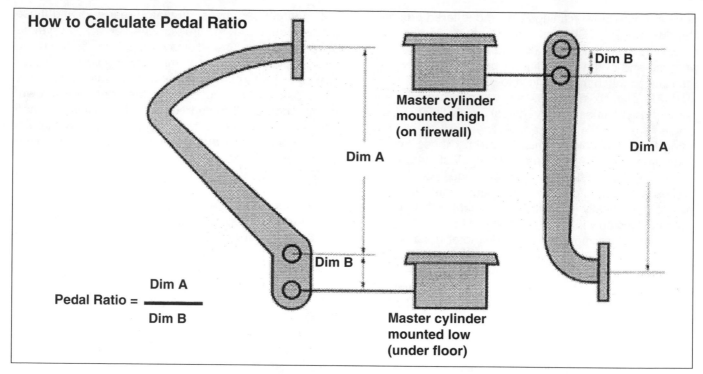

How to Calculate Pedal Ratio

Master cylinder mounted high (on firewall)

Dim A

Dim B

$$\text{Pedal Ratio} = \frac{\text{Dim A}}{\text{Dim B}}$$

Master cylinder mounted low (under floor)

(courtesy of Engineered Components, Inc.)

Here is how you calculate pedal ratio. Low pedal ratio is one of the primary causes of a hard brake pedal.

arm is too short. Your pedal ratio should be a minimum of 5 to 1 and works well around 6 to 1. You can measure this by first taking the length from the end of the pedal arm (about the center of the pad) down to the pedal pivot point. Then divide that number by the length from the pivot point to the master cylinder contact point (see diagram above).

The diameter of the master brake cylinder is also important. You can calculate the total amount of pressure applied to the system by using this formula:

Let's look at an example. If you apply 75 lbs. of force to the pedal and your pedal ratio is 6 to 1 then your top number is 450. If you use a 1-inch diameter master brake cylinder then your bottom number would be 1 x 1 x .785, which is .785. So 450 divided by .785 equals 573 psi. or pounds of pressure in the lines.

Now it is tempting to use a 1 1/8-inch master cylinder thinking more is better and if you push more fluid you will stop the car better, but using this formula you'll see that you actually reduce the amount of pressure to 453 pounds of force. You do indeed displace more fluid, but the fluid is under less pressure. So why not use a smaller cylinder like a 7/8- or 3/4-inch master cylinder? Because you will have more pressure in the system and the pedal will be easier to push.

The problem with this is that the cylinder will displace less brake fluid than needed, so you'll push the pedal all the way to the floor and still not engage the brakes. The bottom line with brakes is that a 1-inch master cylinder is a good rule of thumb, but there are certain wheel cylinders or calipers that require larger or smaller master cylinders. Disc and drum brakes are easier to engage, so it may be a good idea to use a

disc/drum setup on your first car or until you become more familiar with brake systems.

Disc/disc systems may stop the car better, but they are harder to engage and frequently require a brake booster to operate properly. Brake boosters operate off of the vacuum from the engine and most hot rod engines don't create much vacuum due to the racing cams used. So going back to that planning lesson, if you want to use a four-wheel disc setup, it's a good idea to let your engine builder know that you will need 16 to 18 inches of vacuum to run your brake booster.

BRAKE FADE

One of the reasons for total brake failure is "brake fade." There are different kinds of brake fade and they are most commonly found during performance situations like racing or long steep grades. Those of you that watch NASCAR racing may have seen some of the spectacular undercarriage shots of the brakes getting so hot they literally glow red. This really doesn't happen in street cruising, so don't feel like you have to design a $10,000 brake system. Brake pad fade is caused when the pads get so hot the resins begin to liquefy. The melted resin acts as a lubricant, so the pads ride over the rotors. Racers avoid this by using metallic or carbon pads and multiple calipers per wheel. Organic pads are generally recommended for those of us who are not racing.

Most modern cars have semi-metallic pads. Organic pads do wear out faster, but keep in mind that most street rods are not everyday drivers, so the pads aren't used as much. Organic pads grab the rotors

(courtesy of Gibbon Fiberglass Reporductions)

Two things in this photo should give you a clue that the builder intends to put a high-horsepower engine in this car. First, the ladder bar suspension in the rear is ideal for high torque, and four-wheel disc brakes are in place to slow the beast down.

better in normal conditions and require less pedal force to operate. The more metal flake that is in the pad, the more pedal force is required to operate them. Metallic or high-performance pads will only make a hard pedal worse.

Calipers can also cause another type of brake fade. If a caliper gets too hot, the brake fluid can boil and loose its hydraulic properties. This is called "fluid fade." "Deflection" is a term used to describe how calipers stress or flex under load. Metals like steel and cast iron

(courtesy of Gibbon Fiberglass Reproductions

Here is the same frame with engine and transmission. This would be about a $15,000 engine with a blower. The engine, transmission, rear end, rotors and spindles are frame colored for added detail.

flex the least, but absorb and retain heat. Aluminum and magnesium will flex more, but dissipate heat much faster than steel. For everyday use, cast-iron is affordable and works fine, but the exotic metal calipers are offered for racing applications.

One way to reduce fluid fade is to use different kinds of brake fluid. Dot 3 is the standard and works well for most applications. It has a few drawbacks, the first of which is that it boils at high temperatures, which means it can be bad for racing. It also absorbs or attracts water and the only solution for this is to replace it when it starts to look dark brown.

Perhaps the most frustrating thing about Dot 3 is that it is an excellent paint stripper. If you get a leak, it will easily strip the paint off any surface it sits on.

Silicon or Dot 5 fluid is different. It resists water, doesn't boil, and doesn't attack paint. It seemed like a miracle when it came out, and in the 1980s and early '90s everybody was switching to the stuff. A bizarre incident happend while I was managing a paint shop. We, too, made the switch and really liked the Dot 5, until one day an employee spilled a quart of it on the floor in the back of the shop. We cleaned it up the best we could and didn't think much of it again. Shortly thereafter, we began having severe paint problems. We were getting fish eyes all over the place and couldn't get rid of them until I started to remember that silicon and paint don't mix. No one ever told me that silicon could go airborne like that, but it does. It was so difficult cleaning the silicon out of the shop that I banned anything that had silicon in it from that day forward. That means brake fluid, polishing compounds, lubricants, sealers, etc. Unless you race, Dot 3 is just fine by me. Whichever you pick, do not mix the two as they are not compatible and the seals in the system will fail.

By working with a professional to plan your first brake system, you should have brakes that are both easy to use and safe.

Chapter 6

Fiberglass Bodies

Some of the most beautiful cars around are fiberglass-bodied hot rods, but there are some things about them that can be surprising or disappointing to the newcomer. I think most people expect them to be as easy to put together as the plastic models we built as children, but they are not. In fact, most of the failed or abandoned hot rod projects start out as fiberglass kits.

When we hear "kit," we expect it to be 100 percent complete, and all we will have to do is open the crate, read the directions and start putting the thing together. Expectations seem to be that in a few weekends, you'll be driving your new kit car down the road. Very few manufacturers have a step-by-step guide on paper. When you buy a kit, what arrives are the basic body parts only. I've attended numerous car shows and sometimes give "how-to" lectures. I couldn't begin to count how many stories I've listened to over the years concerning failed kit projects and every builder seems to conclude that the kit manufacturer "ripped me off!" However, the real reason why these projects failed is poor planning and false expectations.

WHAT'S IN A KIT?

Fiberglass-bodied hot rods are kits cars, plain and simple. There are hundreds of kit car manufacturers making everything from old Duesenbergs to futuristic space cars. There are dozens of hot rod body manufacturers and the prices of their kits vary significantly. Naturally, we look at the low-cost kits and say, "All 1932 Fords are equal, so why not go with the lowest bidder?" The simple answer is, we get what we pay for and all kits are not equal. The lowest-cost solution may work for the government when it builds bridges, but it rarely works for us street rodders. You should expect that the kit is a body and nothing more.

Most hot rods will have some 3,000 to 6,000 parts and most body kits have just a few dozen. Don't expect neat little packages containing all the nuts and bolts you need for the entire car, although some manufacturers offer this as an option for a fair price and I highly recommend it. Most kit car manufacturers do not build the chassis themselves, but the better ones have established relationships with chassis builders and also offer a semi-complete chassis as an option. The advantage in purchasing this option is that these contractors understand the little "quirks" of the kit, which is very helpful. They usually know where to put the body mounts and brake or gas peddles. You will save very little money trying to build the basic chassis yourself.

The electrical wiring harness can be another challenge. Always ask if the kit builder offers this as an option. If they don't, they should be able to point you to someone

(courtesy of Gibbon Fiberglass Reproductions)

Most of the finishing parts — doors, headlights, wheels, etc. — do not come with a kit. Ask your kit manufacturer which parts are included in its kits.

The light-colored areas along the ceiling and walls are oak reinforcements. This provides both reinforcement and easy tack areas for upholstery.

(courtesy of Gibbon Fiberglass Reproductions)

that has it. The better manufacturers offer all kinds of supplementary kits, like door handles, bezels, glass, gauges, etc. In other words, there is the basic kit on one hand and another kit that has all the parts you really need.

It is important to ask questions about the kit. The danger here is that a hot rod builder may have a budget for $7,000 and get excited to find out that the kit is only $5,000. After the purchase, they discover the kit requires another $15,000 in parts to complete. Understanding what is included before the purchase is crucial because most are nonrefundable so you are locked in

as soon as the kit arrives. Looking for the hidden costs will reduce the risk for failure.

Formulate a priced checklist of all the parts that come with the kit as well as the "extras" needed for completion — right down to the gaskets and washers. Sometimes the less-expensive kits have so few parts that they really are more expensive when you make an apples to apples comparison.

The less-expensive kits usually require extensive engineering as well. Common issues seem to revolve around the doors, trunk and hood. I've seen kits that

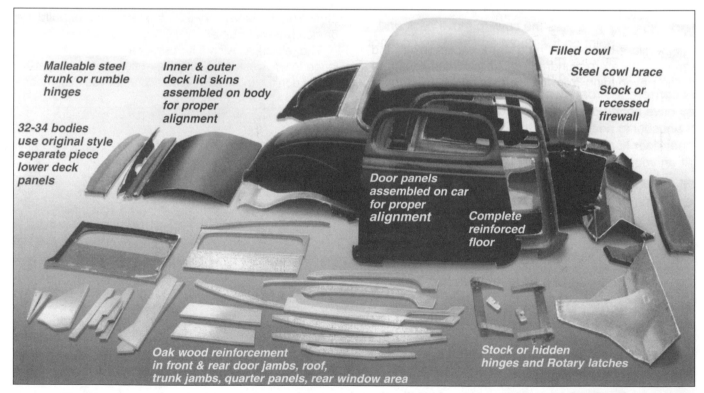

Malleable steel trunk or rumble hinges

Inner & outer deck lid skins assembled on body for proper alignment

32-34 bodies use original style separate piece lower deck panels

Door panels assembled on car for proper alignment

Complete reinforced floor

Filled cowl

Steel cowl brace

Stock or recessed firewall

Oak wood reinforcement in front & rear door jambs, roof, trunk jambs, quarter panels, rear window area

Stock or hidden hinges and Rotary latches

(courtesy of Gibbon Fiberglass Reproductions)

This kit comes with doors and trunk lid assembled on the car. This saves a lot of time in the build process.

You need the body and finished wheels to get your rear end width, but the fiberglass manufacturer only needs the frame to make a custom floor. An inexpensive rolling dolly can be made for the frame to make it easier to move until suspension is added.

(courtesy of Gibbon Fiberglass Reproductions)

provide a body and a pair of doors right out of the mold with no hardware at all. The novice gets one of these kits and then has to figure out how to mount the doors, where to drill the holes and how to make the door hinges from scratch. The better kit manufacturers will offer to deliver the kit with doors and other panels already mounted. This is the best option!

Find out if the manufacturer provides a turn-key option. This means that they build the entire car right down to the paint, chrome, interior, etc. A turn-key kit is essentially a brand new car, ready to go. You just show up, they hand you the keys and you're gone! I recommend that you only

do business with companies that offer turn-key solutions, not because you have to buy it this way, but you would be surprised how many fiberglass companies have never even built their own kit! Chances are, if they haven't built their kit, they will not be a helpful resource for you as you go. You need someone reliable to speak with if you get stuck during the build and need help.

STICK WITH A SOLID COMPANY

Gibbon Fiberglass Reproductions of Darlington, South Carolina, has been manufacturing fiberglass bodies since the early 1970s. We'll use them as an

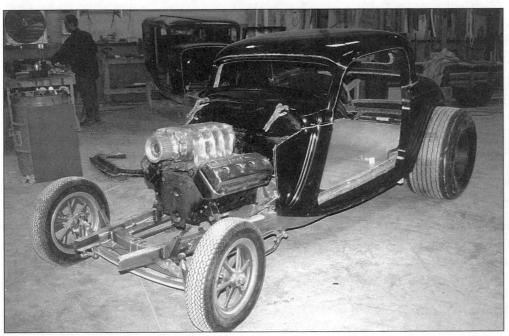

Pro street cars are more difficult to plan in the sense that the manufacturer needs to see the finished wheels and rear suspension in place. The custom floor and wheel wells are made to match the size and position of the tires. A chassis builder familiar with fiberglass can help.

(courtesy of Gibbon Fiberglass Reproductions)

(courtesy of Gibbon Fiberglass Reproductions)

Here is a better view of how the large rear tires affect the back end. With this car, the manufacturer had to design a special trunk to match the tires.

example of how to do things right when it comes to fiberglass bodies.

As with hot rods themselves, fiberglass technology has been constantly refined over the years. One of the challenges in fiberglass is how to deal with expansion and contraction in the material. Both steel and fiberglass expand and contract, but with fiberglass the movement can cause cracking in the body over time. With steel, only the paint will crack. The industry has bounced around this issue over the years, but at one time it was thought that your fiberglass body would be stronger if it had few seams. For a while, bodies were made to be almost one-piece units. The problem with this concept is that there are no places for the body to expand and stress cracks eventually begin to show at the 90-degree corners of the body.

Gibbon builds the body as several mini body parts and bolts them together to form a singular car body, much like the original cars were done. So you have a separate floor, firewall, roof, etc., and then assemble these so that the seams lie in natural expansion areas around the 90-degree locations of the body. The fiberglass panels can be made in different ways. The most common is a hand-laid procedure where fiberglass mat is soaked in resin and laid in the mold in layers. If this is done properly, the fiberglass becomes strong and is usually 3/16 to a 1/4 inch thick.

The inside of the body panels are rarely gel-coated, so be sure to inspect these areas. Improperly laid fiberglass will have frosty white areas where air bubbles or dry fiberglass have accumulated. This fiberglass will be weak and crack easily. Gibbon uses a roller to press the fiberglass properly against the mold to work out the air bubbles and properly saturate all of the fibers.

Fiberglass bodies should have reinforcement inside the body as well. Some companies use steel and others, wood. Gibbon uses both depending on the need. Wood has some advantages in that the pores absorb the resin and bonds with the fiberglass. It also is easy to tack upholstery or screw small fasteners too. Gibbon chooses mostly wood reinforcement, but they use steel in the firewall to support the steering column and door hinges.

Gibbon also offers several key options. First, they will build your floor custom to your frame. This is important, because they provide their kits standard with the doors and trunk lid mounted and adjusted. This service is already included in the price of the kit, so make sure that you compare apples to apples when you shop around. But what good is it to have the body all set up at the factory, only to have a hot rodder start over with the adjustments, because the body doesn't match your frame when it arrives? And how can I ship the finished chassis over to the manufacturer if I need the body to finish the chassis? Well, you can't, but all they need is the frame, not the whole chassis.

AFTER YOUR KIT ARRIVES

When your kit arrives, inspect all of the parts and make sure that none of the fiberglass is damaged and

(courtesy of Gibbon Fiberglass Reproductions)

When the kit arrives, lay out all of the components and check to see if any parts are missing.

that all of the parts are there. If this build project lasts a few years, it isn't fair to call the manufacturer two years after purchase and claim a part is missing. Lay the parts out and see how they fit together. Most manufacturers will include a manual stating their advice for the build. Read this manual thoroughly before any work begins.

Fiberglass doesn't cure with time, it cures with heat and it will cure to the highest temperature it is exposed to. Many rodders have found out the hard way that a car gets real hot out in the sun. I remember inspecting a car in

west Texas one summer. It was the usual 107 degrees in the shade, and I made the mistake of leaning against the car. Immediately, I jumped back in pain. The "friend" I was with got a good chuckle out of it, but I had a first-degree burn in just that second's time. Judging on how quickly I got burned, I guess the car's surface was between 160 and 170 degrees. This was a light-colored car, too. The darker the color, the hotter the surface will get.

To test this more accurately, I rolled a red car I had recently painted outside to heat up. It was around 70 degrees and I wanted to cure the paint faster. After the

Fiberglass doesn't cure with time, it cures with heat and will cure to the highest temperature it is exposed to. When your fiberglass body arrives be sure to set all your pieces out in the sun.

(courtesy of Gibbon Fiberglass Reproductions)

car had been sitting for an hour, I put a thermometer against the paint and it read 155!

Most manufacturers cure the fiberglass up to 110 degrees, but that is not enough. As fiberglass cures, the surface gets slightly bumpy or orange peeled. A lot of guys don't understand this until the car is finished and is being shown for the first time. At the beginning of the show the car looks great, and by the time the show is over, the car's paint looks rough. This is because they were curing the fiberglass for the first time and it changed texture in the process. This will happen even if the fiberglass is many years old.

To avoid this, take all of your fiberglass parts and place them out in the sun on a hot day. This can certainly affect the planning process if you live in a cool climate, and laying parts outside in winter won't accomplish much. It is important to bolt all of the parts to the body before the curing process because the parts form to the body some while curing. The surface should feel hot to the touch, but if you have doubts, purchase an inexpensive candy thermometer and take a reading. The surface needs to get to 150 degrees or more. Most manufacturers will also encourage you to avoid dark colors like black or navy blue on fiberglass cars for this same heat and curing issue. After the curing process is complete, you can begin the rough build.

CLEANING UP THE BODY

Your next step is to perform the rough shaping and cutting of the fiberglass. If you remember your plastic model days, you had to clean up and trim down the seams of the model. This is because there was excess plastic where the part touched the mold. Fiberglass is no different. The seams where the mold bolts together will leave extra material on the body and this excess is called flashing lines.

Gibbon repairs these for you, but that is not the norm in the industry, so these lines will need to be addressed

first on most kits. With an abrasive disc or dual action sander, grind the seams so that 1/2 inch on either side of the flashing line has been ground back and about 1/16 to 1/8 of an inch deep. The exposed area should be blown clean with compressed air. Body work techniques are addressed further in Chapter 8, but once the seams are cleaned, apply a thin coat of body filler along all of the exposed fiberglass and sand flush once it has cured.

All of your first work is just a rough go-around, so I would feel comfortable using power tools to sand your filler in this stage and an 80 or 120 grit should work fine. All of the gel-coat over the entire vehicle needs to be lightly sanded with the same grit paper to break the surface up for proper primer adhesion.

THE ROUGH BUILD

The rough build is really similar to that involving the chassis, but with a new emphasis. We need to mount the body to the frame and go through the process of mounting the body parts like fenders, hood, doors, etc. Many fiberglass manufacturers will ship the body to you with doors and trunk lid installed and if they do, do not remove these! Go ahead and go through the build process to finish the chassis with suspension, drive train and wheels as in Chapter 4. All of the parts must line up and mate flush to the body. Bolt everything in place, including the fenders and running boards.

One of the characteristics of fiberglass is you cannot tighten the fasteners as hard as you can with steel, and this may feel strange at first. We have been told most of our lives to tighten everything down as hard as possible, but if you do that on fiberglass, you will crack it. The cracking or crushed effect is called "starring." One recommendation Kyle Bond at Gibbon Fiberglass has, is to use nylock nuts to secure any fiberglass parts, such as fenders. The normal pressure needed to compress a split washer is enough to create starring, so Bond uses the same bolt, flat

Note the flashing lines near the firewall and above the windshield. This manufacturer finishes these for customers, but most companies send the product out like this.

(courtesy of Gibbon Fiberglass Reproductions)

(courtesy of Gibbon Fiberglass Reproductions)

Don't install the dash until all of the holes in the firewall have been measured and cut.

washers on both sides, no metal lock washers and nylock nuts instead. Less torque is needed with nylon lock nuts to secure the parts. You also want to distribute the force out over the largest area possible, so the larger the flat washer, the better.

There should be few, if any, holes on the firewall and floor. I guess it could be considered lazy for the manufacturer not to cut the holes themselves, but every kit car is different and every chassis has mounts in different places. All that would happen is they would cut a bunch of holes that wouldn't be used, so the industry makes the safe play and leaves it up to you.

You need a Dremmel, cut-off wheel or Roto-zip tool to make these cuts. The first cuts are always a little nerve-racking, so make them in low visibility-areas like the gas pedal or stick shift. The cool thing about fiberglass is, that even if you cut the hole in the wrong place, you can glue the part back in place with resin. Fiberglass is very forgiving in that regard.

You usually need to cut holes for wiring, gearshift, windshield wipers, bumper brackets, headlights, taillights and blinkers. The best way to avoid a mistake is to start with a small hole and cut outward until you have the hole the way you like it. This method works well for

(courtesy of Gibbon Fiberglass Reproductions)

Fiberglass kits do not come with pre-cut holes in the firewall. This gives car builders more flexibility in selecting mounting locations.

(courtesy of Gibbon Fiberglass Reproductions)

This builder chose to perform a rough build of the interior. All of the steps in custom building overlap each other. This rough build helps determine if the steering column and shift lever are in the right place.

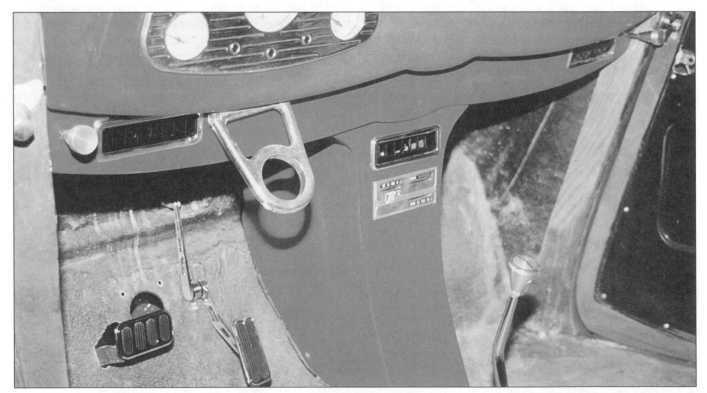

(courtesy of Gibbon Fiberglass Reproductions)

Note how precisely this brake pedal hole has been cut. One way to get a smaller hole is to disconnect the pedal arm from the master cylinder and lower the arm down into the hole, rather than cutting a hole.

(courtesy of Gibbon Fiberglass Reproductions)

Not all builders mount the hood during the rough build process, but you need to know if the engine will clear before any painting is done.

Some hood adjustments will be simple, as is the case with this early Ford. Others will take more patience, like with this '55 Chevy (left).

(courtesy of Gibbon Fiberglass Reproductions and Interiors by Shannon)

(courtesy of Street Rods by Michael)

Some kits offer a lift-off top at no extra cost. A power convertible top adds about $2,500 to the project cost.

the pedals and gearshift where some educated guessing is used to locate the proper spot. However, many of the holes are used to mount parts like the headlights. You can reduce errors by making a paper template of the headlight housing first and then trace the outline on the fiberglass before any cutting is done.

It's a good idea to make all of your cuts and mount all of the pieces before priming. The edges of all the parts like fenders, hood, trunk lid and doors need to be worked too. The fenders are perhaps the easiest. The excess fiberglass from the molding process needs to be trimmed off and all edges sanded smooth. The other parts are more involved. The body should already be bolted to the frame, then the doors, trunk lid and hood should be mounted and lined up.

Most manufacturers do not install the hood, so you will have to do this yourself. Hoods on the earliest Fords are fairly easy to do, but most other hoods have two major adjustments. First, the hinges need to be placed properly on the vertical plane. Usually this is obvious in

the sense that with the hood closed, the hood rests above the cowl at the rear or strikes the cowl because the hinges are too low. It is difficult to get the hinges wrong on the horizontal plane, but one symptom of this is, the hood will bind and not want to close.

Make the hinge-to-firewall adjustments first, and then check to see if the hood is lined up on the hinges properly. With the hood closed, it should be centered and have a uniform gap all along its perimeter. You may need to make adjustments on all the panels. After these adjustments, you may notice a few areas where the gap is not uniform. This is because the hood, doors and trunk lids have not been trued up to the body. The goal of the truing process is to have a uniform gap in all of the seams. The truing process is done after the surfaces have had their first coats of primer applied.

Using the techniques in Chapter 8, clean the surfaces to be primed and apply enough epoxy primer to cover the surface. This should take about two coats. Once it's dry, apply several coats of urethane high-build

(courtesy of Gibbon Fiberglass Reproductions)

Rough bodywork has begun on this Gibbon Viper. Note the work being done to the rear of this side engine panel. It is being sanded down so it lies flush with the body. This type of fitting is key to beautiful paint.

primer. With the panels closed, check the gap along the perimeter of all the panels. For example, if the gap at the top of the door is 1/16 inch and the bottom is 5/16 inch, then you know that the door has not been adjusted properly. However, if it is a uniform gap close to 3/16 inch all the way around with the exception of a few places, then the door edge needs to be trued. This is done by taking a sanding block and lightly filing the edges so the high spots (or tight gaps) are removed. You should be left with a smooth, uniform gap. The body is now ready for the standard bodywork process. The bodywork should be done with the body still mounted to the frame. It's a good idea to remove the finished wheels and drive train to keep them clean. You

may want to wrap the frame and suspension in plastic as well.

Most standard kits do not include any kind of trim. Trim can include taillight and headlight bezels, chrome window frames, door handles, latches, as well as any stainless or aluminum trim you might find on a stock car. Most hot rods lack a lot of these parts anyway, but it's nice to have some chrome accents on the exterior to set off the paint. Most of the better kit manufacturers will offer an assortment of trim options. Finally, it is difficult for a manufacturer to offer a custom interior kit, so the interior will have to be built from scratch. Most kits cost between $6,000 and $9,000 with a wide assortment of options and accessories adding an optional $5,000 more.

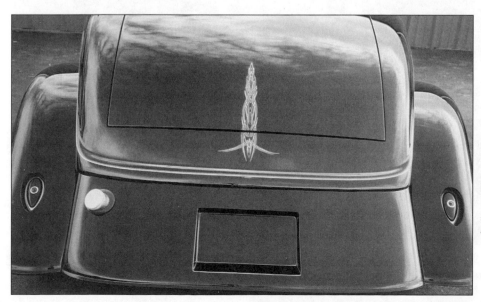

This trunk lid has been trued properly. Notice that the gap is uniform around the entire perimeter. The taillights have been recessed, too. Frenched lights are similar, but lack the chrome bezels and are flush to the body.

(courtesy of TL Rod and Custom)

Chapter 7

Metal Bodies

More effort is required to build steel-bodied custom cars than fiberglass ones. Your plan must address rust or collision damage as well as any custom modifications that will need to be done. Fiberglass bodies are new, so they won't be rusty or dented. They already have modifications like chopped roofs or hidden door handles. Steel bodies are a different matter.

Every potential donor car you look at will have some degree of rust. Small amounts of oxidation can be found on brand new cars, but most donor hot rod bodies are well over 60 years old and have been stored outside. The extent and location of the rust is the real issue. When you bought your last car, how long did it take to get its first dent? Think about how long these cars have been around. The steel will have small dents — this isn't a big deal. But has the car ever been wrecked?

Understanding the costs involved in repairing and modifying metal before the donor body is even purchased is key to a good plan. As you shop around for the right body, make a tally of all the expenses needed to bring the metal to a "like new" status. It is very tempting when you find the right make and model advertised for a $1,000 to say to yourself, "Hey, this is $9,000 less than a fiberglass kit, what a deal!" Add to this $1,500 to disassemble the body, $1,000 to strip the metal, $2,000 to repair rusted floor pans, $3,500 to chop the top, $500 to replace a damaged fender and so on. This tally of expense is the actual cost of the car.

So how do you know how much detail or finishing to ask for? The answer depends on the budget and whether you plan to show the car. Show cars are highly

(courtesy of Interiors by Shannon)

Details like this custom hood hinge and chopped top are already provided on a fiberglass car. With metal bodies, however, it's up to the builder. Each detail will have to be planned out an modified by the builder.

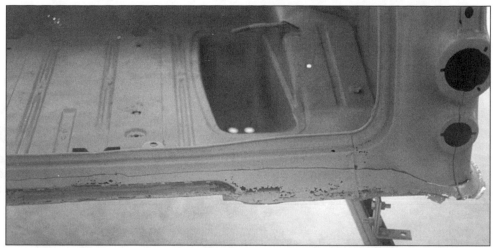

The rear bumper covered most of this rust damage. The entire rear of the car looks like "Swiss cheese." Expect repairs like this to run in the thousands of dollars.

detailed, and can have $40,000 or more in metalwork expense. Most of the bill is wrapped up in subtle details. Judges have a trained eye for detail and can have discerning tastes. Cars now seem to be judged under a microscope and some custom car fans complain that judging at car shows has gotten to be too picky. The criticism may be valid, and the winning show cars seem to have gotten out of reach for the average enthusiast.

As you seek out professionals for different stages of the project, take time to fully explain your intentions. Be careful with some of the terminology and jargon you hear, especially "show car." To say that you are building a show car to a professional may be interpreted far from the meaning you intend. The term "show car" to a professional often means that you have a budget of $100,000 or more and that the car will be shown in national competition. The shop owner will see the car as future advertising for the shop and assume that it needs to be a masterpiece. Show cars are rarely driven. Instead, they are usually hauled in a trailer from one place to the other. I know of too many stories where a novice customer dropped off a car with one intention and panicked when they saw the bill. The best way to avoid this is to simply tell the shop what your budget is and what you intend to spend. Withholding this information can only lead to misunderstandings later on.

RUST IS BIG FACTOR

Rust is perhaps the most frustrating concern. It can be traced to areas that were poorly prepped during

This is typical of a car out in the field. The car is difficult to inspect because of the thick grass under the car and spare parts cover the floor on top. Take the extra time to pull the parts out and inspect everything. If the owner has a problem with it, walk away. All kinds of parts are missing, the back right corner of the car is smashed in and the floor is rusted through in many places. This car should be avoided unless it is the only one available.

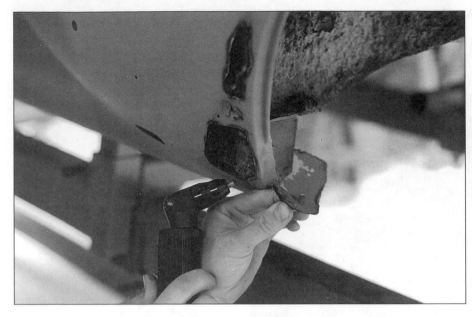

Stainless molding can hide rust at the time of sale. Several holes were found under the stone guards. The rusted areas are cut out first.

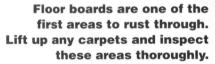

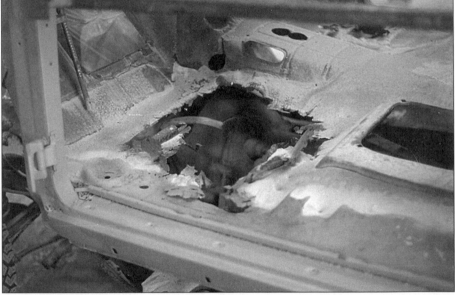

Floor boards are one of the first areas to rust through. Lift up any carpets and inspect these areas thoroughly.

Paint bubbles and flakes off when metal rusts from the inside out. These areas usually reveal rust holes when the metal is stripped.

Old cars that have been driven on salty roads usually have rust around the wheel wells and floor. This car's frame is even rusted through. There may be as much as $20,000 in rust repair on this body. There are others out there — keep looking.

the paint process or areas the factory left unprotected. Rust progresses in stages starting with mild surface oxidation. As the damage continues, pits form and eventually turn into holes. These holes vary from pin size to more than a foot depending on the situation. One of the frustrating aspects of rust is that it can't always be seen at the time of purchase. Mild surface oxidation is difficult to detect under faded paint work. Interior trim, bumpers and moldings often conceal damaged areas from view. Rust is often found under factory undercoating and isn't seen until the car is stripped. Donor vehicles frequently find themselves in overgrown fields so the underside of the car can be difficult to inspect. Most owners are not going to allow you to remove portions of the car to give you full access, so a complete inspection may be impossible, but the more time spent during the inspection the better. Bring a sheet of cardboard to lay on as well as a magnet, flashlight and telescoping mirror.

It's a given that vehicles driven in northern and coastal states are exposed to salt and are most likely poor choices for your project. When inspecting the body pay close attention to the wheel wells, floor, trunk and firewall. These areas are exposed to water the most often. The greater the degree of oxidation, the more expensive the project will be. A point is eventually reached where the cost of the repair exceeds the value of the car, so it pays to be selective.

AVOID SALVAGE PROJECTS

Small dents are not an issue, but collision damage repairs can be very expensive. Replacement panels are not always available like they are on modern cars, which means the body will have to be disassembled at the welds and custom patch panels made to replace damaged metal. With labor rates of $50 to $75 an hour, collision work can easily run $10,000 or more. My recommendation is to avoid a car that has been wrecked or has seriously deteriorated.

METALWORK CONSIDERATIONS

Steel body modifications can be another costly process. Chopping, frenching and channeling are techniques that require skill to complete. If you do not feel comfortable with your metal working skill, you will need to enlist the help of a professional. All of these modifications have various levels of detail that can be added.

Chopping a top will typically run around $3,500. This sum will pay for the job to be done right by a professional, but the degree of detail and metal finishing will be very basic. There is an infinite number of extra details that can be added to car body. These details are often subtle, but are very time consuming. For example, windows can be set at different angles, flat glass can be changed to curved, door pillar posts can change shape or angle, etc. All of these details add to and help define the overall theme of the car.

The degree that metalwork can be finished out is also variable. When custom metalwork began, both tools and techniques were limited. Most panels were brazed or welded in place in such a way that the panels warped. Modern polyester body fillers were not available, so large quantities of lead were used to smooth the shape of the car out and cover up seams. This is where the term "lead sled" comes from. Today, metal work is much more refined. TIG welders use a foot pedal to adjust the heat so the welder only has to apply the minimum needed to melt the rod. Expert metal finishers know how to shape, file and weld metal so no lead or body filler is needed. The weld is laid a little at a time and the metal is tapped with a pick hammer and repeatedly filed to get a smooth shape that needs little or no bodywork to finish. This process is time consuming, but isn't mandatory. Some body filler will not reduce the quality of the paint or bodywork.

STRIPPING THE BODY

The first step in working with metal bodies is to strip them down to remove rust, paint and tar. The stripping

Sandblasting is the most versatile stripping method and can be used on any of the reinforced steel areas. However, enough heat is produced to warp exterior panels.

(courtesy of the Eastwood Company)

technique varies depending on what type of metal you are working with. The vast majority of cars are made out of steel and they can be stripped in a variety of ways. Abrasive methods are the most popular with media blasting being at the top of the list.

Sandblasting is just one of many types of media blasting. Walnut shells, soda powder, graphite, plastic and glass beads are just a few of the choices. Different media is used depending on the type of metal being stripped. Sand is the least expensive and frequently used on steel. Most sandblasters cost around $400 and are ideal for stripping both old paint and rust. Sandblasting requires a lot of compressed air so most of the small air compressors struggle to keep up. The job can be done with a small compressor, but you usually have to blast for a few minutes and stop as the pressure builds back up. Sandblasting creates enough heat to warp the outside panels and should not be used there, but it is perfect for firewalls, jams, trunks, floors or any other reinforced piece of steel.

Sandblasting should not be used on exterior panels because the heat will warp the panel. Abrasive discs and sanders work well as a substitute. It helps to move the disc around and try not to concentrate in one place.

(courtesy of the Eastwood Company)

Grinders can be used to strip paint on outside panels. The same tool can be used to polish paint as well.

(courtesy of the Eastwood Company)

Abrasive disks can be fitted to electric drills or die grinders to reach the tighter places.

(courtesy of the Eastwood Company)

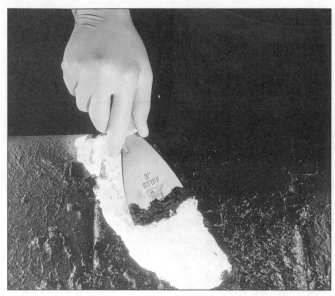

(courtesy of the Eastwood Company)

Paint stripper can be good for loosening thick paint before grinding or sandblasting. It is also gentle enough to be used on aluminum.

A word of warning: Inhaling the dirty air and silica dust caused by sandblasting can lead the breathing disorder known as silicosis. Always wear a helmet, gloves, suit and respirator while sandblasting.

Grinders and abrasive disks are also used to cut old paint and rust off. A grinder with a 36-grit pad works well on outside panels and cuts paint quickly. There should not be a problem with the panels warping as long as you constantly move around the panel to dis-tribute the heat. The grinder will take off good metal, too, so as soon as you see steel, stop and switch to a dual-action sander with an 80-grit pad. An assortment of wire wheels and abrasive disks are offered as drill or die grinder attachments for places the large grinders can't get to. A good grinder costs around $135 and can be used as a buffer, too.

Chemical stripping is another method at your disposal. "Chem dip" is the term used to describe the method of dipping the steel down into an acid bath to remove paint and rust. Some companies have chemical tanks so large that the entire body can be submerged. The process costs around $1,300 for a complete car body. The advantage with this method is that the rust removing chemical gets into all the cracks and places you can't see. The problem with chemical dip is that you have to haul the car around and not all areas have a shop with this service. Also, the metal will begin to rust again fairly quickly, so you must be prepared to prime the entire body soon after it is removed from the acid.

Old-fashioned paint stripper is another chemical that is commonly used. Paint stripper will not remove rust, but is ideal for removing multiple coats of paint. The fumes are pretty noxious, so make sure you use a respirator and gloves to protect your skin. When working with aluminum, chemical strippers are a must. The metal is just too soft for abrasive means.

Which method is the best? The answer is all of the above, depending on the situation. If a car is extremely rusty, chemical dip may be your best solution. I don't use this method very often because I recommend avoiding cars with that much damage in the first place. Sandblasting seems to work the best for the majority of situations, along with a grinder for the outside panels. Should the paint buildup be excessive, time can be saved by loosening up the coats with traditional paint remover before the sandblasting takes place.

TACKLING RUST

Some degree of rust repair is unavoidable. The stripping process will remove surface oxidation and small pits. It will also help you assess the extent of the rust. Many of the areas you thought were pits actually turn to holes after they have been stripped. The smaller holes of 3/8 inch and less can be welded up. The excess weld can be ground smooth to complete the repair.

As the holes get larger, patch panels will need to be made and welded in place. The rusted area is first cut out and a new piece is made out of stock sheet metal. As with any welding on a car body, the piece is first tacked

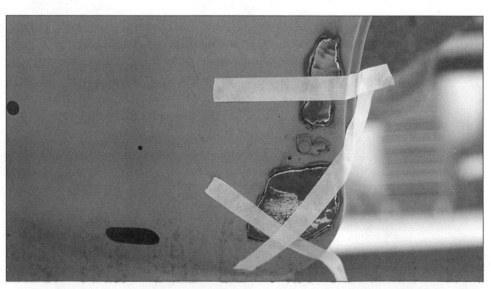

Patch panels are made and cut to fit. Tape or magnets can be used to hold the metal in place before tack welding.

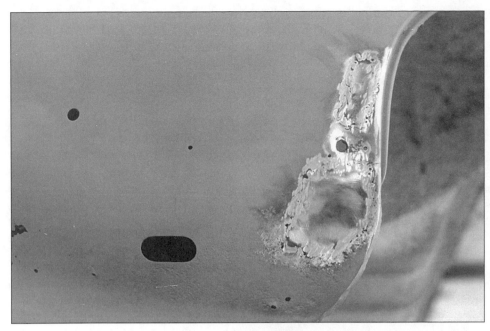

With the welding complete, the welds can be ground flush. Hold a light behind the panel and check to see if any pin holes exist in the weld. In this case, the tiny black spots are holes in the weld. These holes need to be welded up before moving on. The surface may not feel
perfectly smooth, but
that will be fixed in the bodywork phase.

This vehicle had rust damage on both front floor pans. The original spot welds have been drilled without damaging the braces under the floor. The donor floor pan has been removed from a parts car and welded in place. A job like this runs between $1,500 and $2,500. If the firewall, trunk and wheel wells are also damaged, the entire rust repair could exceed $10,000.

into place and welded slowly into place 1/4 inch at a time. Between each small weld, stop and cool the area down with compressed air. This technique keeps the surface of the steel cool and reduces the risk of warping the panel. As the holes continue to get larger, the strategy for repair changes. For example, if the entire lower portion of a door is rusted through, it may be more economical to spend $300 and buy a new door.

It's common to find floor pans with holes 10 inches wide or more. This happens when cars aren't stored properly and water is allowed to collect inside. The most challenging aspect of floor pan replacement is removing the old pan without damaging the surrounding braces or floor supports. To master this type of repair, it helps to understand how cars are manufactured.

Steel bodies start out as flat sheet metal. These sheets are stamped into shapes and are spot welded together to form basic parts and these parts are in turn spot welded together to form the body. Looking at our floor example, inner and outer rocker panel sheets are spot welded together to form a boxed rocker panel. Individual sheets are stamped into the floor pans and laid on top of the rockers. Various braces and floor supports are stamped out and spot welded under the floor and so on. All of these individual components are spot welded together to create the floor. As the floor moves down the assembly line, other similarly created parts are welded on, like the firewall, fenders and roof. This process can be reversed, right down to hammering all the individual parts back to flat sheet metal.

If a floor pan is to be replaced, the spot welds holding the pan to the rockers and floor braces must be located and separated. Special drill bits can be purchased that drill out these small welds. Once all of the welds holding the panel in place have been removed, the panel will come right out. Replacement panels can be custom made or obtained from donor cars. Trim the replacement panel to fit and weld in place using a spot welder or weld up the drilled out holes.

You may find yourself in a situation where you remove one rusted panel, only to find the adjacent panels and bracing to be rusted through as well. Professionals call this "Swiss cheese" because you remove one slice with holes in it, just to see the same thing on the next. You may end up drilling out 50 welds or more just for one floor pan and it is tedious, time-consuming work. Add to this rocker panels, floor bracing and trunk flooring and you have a major commitment on your hands. If the holes are small, they can be welded up and ground smooth. However, if the next layer of steel has rusted to the point that it needs to be replaced, you may be fighting a loosing battle. It is very rare that one, isolated brace or support has rusted through. Usually, if you find Swiss cheese in one place, it is all over the car and the expense in repairing this is greater than the car is worth.

If you are committed to a body that is rusted to this degree, there is one fiberglass technique that may help you. Providing that the metal still has structural integrity, fiberglass can be set on the inside of a brace or rocker panel to give the metal strength and fill large rusted spots.

Let's use a rocker panel as an example. The rocker is the boxed piece of metal that runs down the length of the body just below the door. There is a rocker on either side of the car and it reinforces the body like the frame rails do. Some rocker panels have holes cut in them during the manufacturing process, and these holes allow water and salt to get up inside the body. In time, the rockers can deteriorate to the point where hundreds of little rust holes run down their entire length. To use fiberglass properly, access holes will need to be cut on the top side of the rocker. Both the inside and outside of the rocker need to be sandblasted and primed in epoxy primer. This will keep the metal from rusting again. Once dry, several layers of fiberglass resin and mat are laid on the inside of the rocker. Masking tape or wax paper can be used to keep the resin from dripping through the holes and onto the floor. Once dry, the excess resin can be ground flush on the outside of the rocker with a dual-action sander and primed again. This technique builds strength and fills the holes at the same time and is about four times faster than welding. The preferred solution would be to replace or weld up the metal, but fiberglass works well on a budget.

BODY MODIFICATIONS

With all the rust and major damage behind us, we can revisit the various body modifications found in custom work. The most common body modifications are chopping, channeling and frenching. Many of the modifications were first done to lower the car to the ground, reduce wind resistance and increase speed.

Chopping is a technique used to lower the roof of a car several inches and is one of the most popular modifications done today. Channeling removes the metal on the floor and firewall that is in contact with the frame. The entire body is lowered around the frame and welded in place. This modification lowers the body to the ground without modifying the chassis. Frenching is more of a decorative or styling change rather than function. To create a custom look, tail light or turn signal housings can be removed, and the lenses grafted right into the body. This can be done with almost any exterior bezel or handle to clean up the body lines and get almost any custom design.

Another way rodders alter the appearance of a car is to build new panels from scratch. Famous examples of this would be some of the cars made for television, like the Batmobile. This car started with a stock body and then new panels were made for it to give it a truly unique look. Most street rods are not that radical, but custom-made hoods and hood panels are quite common. To understand custom metal work better, our next stop takes us to Iron Mountain, Michigan. Dan Kemppainen at Kemps Rod and Custom builds everything from show quality street rods to their own limited production models, like the "Kempster." The techniques used to chop tops changes depending on the contour of the body. The next series of photographs show the chop process for three common body styles: '50 Mercury, '37 Chevy and '29 Model A.

(courtesy of Kemps Rod and Restoration)

The key to any successful modification is referencing. Whenever the dimensions of the body change, reference points are needed to make sure the body goes back together straight and level. In the case of chopping a top, the reference points are needed at the top and bottom of the window frames around the vehicle. The front window will get reference points at the top and bottom of either side of the window frame. A carpenter's square is first clamped perpendicular to the floor, and then the top and bottom reference lines are drawn on masking tape. It is important for the marks be in line with each other. Take a top-to-bottom measurement between the lines. The distance between these two lines is exactly 15 1/2 inches. Logic follows that if we want a 3-inch chop, then the measurement should be 12 1/2 inches just before we weld the window post together. Reference points are placed and measurements taken on all of the windows and doors around the car. The front window and door pillar post is called the "A" pillar. Notice how precisely the 3-inch areas have been marked off. Ball point pens are used to scribe the lines instead of felt markers. Felt markers are too thick and leave too much room for error.

(courtesy of Kemps Rod and Restoration)

The reference lines on the tape can clearly be seen. For added detail, the angle of the door window frames will be changed. Scribe lines on either side of this B pillar post mark the areas to be removed. A paper template is made so the lines can be duplicated on the driver's side.

Once 3 inches have been removed from the pillars, the entire roof will shift forward a couple of inches to mate back to the A pillar. To compensate for this forward shift the rear window frame will be leaned down to make up the gap at the rear of the roof.

Cut lines are scribed so the rear window frame can be removed as one piece.

Before the roof pillars are cut, the door posts are removed. This will allow the roof to drop down. The driver's side reference lines can be seen on the front window frame. The roof provides substantial support and rigidity for the body — so much so that convertibles usually have a reinforced frame to compensate for the lost support. When the roof is cut loose, the body has a tendency to warp or change shape. It is important for the body to be bolted to the frame before any cutting begins.

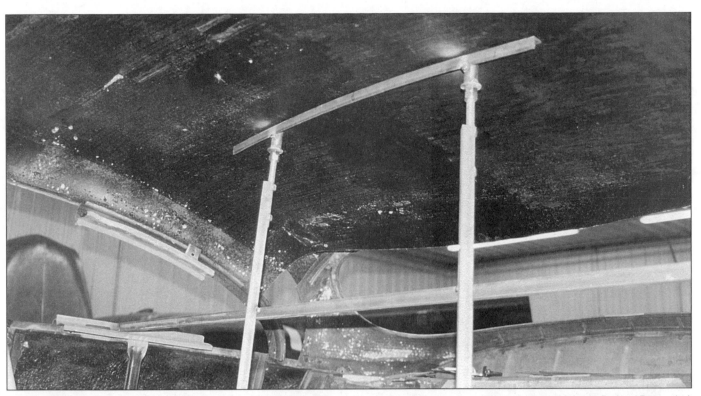

(courtesy of Kemps Rod and Restoration)

A typical roof weighs 200 lbs. or more, so a couple of adjustable roof supports are built out of scrap metal. This tool will support the roof while the posts are cut and hold it in place when it is time to weld.

(courtesy of Kemps Rod and Restoration)

As the roof drops down, the rear quarter glass will change shape. The window channels are cut away before the roof drops.

(courtesy of Kemps Rod and Restoration)

The roof is cut free at the "A" pillar posts and across the top of the rear window. A cutoff wheel and die grinder are used to make the cut. Weld gaps need to be kept to a minimum so a cutoff wheel thickness of 1/32 inch or less should be used. Once free, the roof is slid forward to mate with the "A" pillar.

(courtesy of Kemps Rod and Restoration)

The reference lines are all checked to make sure the 3-inch chop is consistent all the way around. You can start to see how far the rear window will tilt down to mate with the roof.

(courtesy of Kemps Rod and Restoration)

The rear window channels are notched so they fit flush with the body again.

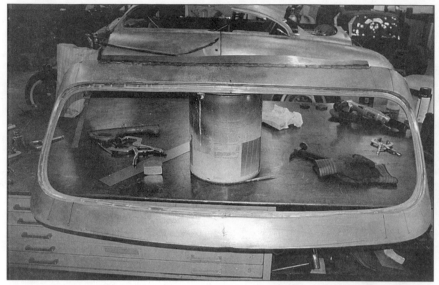

The entire rear window frame is cut loose. A test fitting of the frame at its new angle revealed that a 1/2-inch gap still exists between the roof and frame. A strip of metal is added to the top edge of the frame and will be trimmed to fill the gap.

(courtesy of Kemps Rod and Restoration)

The area between the trunk and rear window is called the deck. The original shape of the deck has an angular transition for the window. After the chop, the window lays down too far and a decision is made to remove this angle and have flat metal all the way across the deck. Relief cuts are made so the trunk portion and the window portion of the deck line up.

(courtesy of Kemps Rod and Restorationl)

(courtesy of Kemps Rod and Restoration)

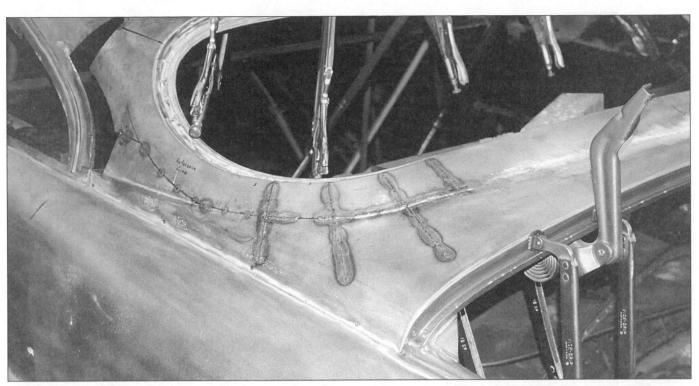

(courtesy of Kemps Rod and Restoration)

With the reference points checked, the rear window can be tacked in place. As the welds are filled, make sure the metal is not getting hot enough to warp the surrounding area. This is accomplished by welding small spots at a time and cooling the metal with compressed air between each weld.

(courtesy of Kemps Rod and Restoration)

Custom pieces of flat metal will be made to fill the side gaps.

(courtesy of Kemps Rod and Restoration)

The transition between the roof and window frame is smoothed out the same way as the deck was done. Notice how the relief cuts are much longer. It is very easy to warp the roof with cuts of this length. Several reinforcements were welded from the doorjambs to the floor.

(courtesy of Kemps Rod and Restoration)

Filler panels were manufactured out of stock metal and hammered to shape. There were so many relief cuts in the corners that it made more sense to graft in new metal than to weld up a dozen individual lines.

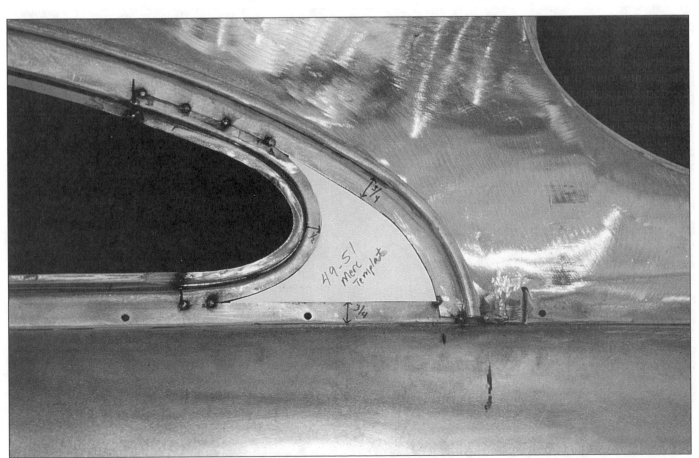

(courtesy of Kemps Rod and Restoration)

The shape for the rear quarter glass is determined and a template is made so both sides of the car match.

(courtesy of Kemps Rod and Restoration)

A piece of the original channel is trimmed and shaped using a stretching tool from Eastwood. It is tacked in place and checked.

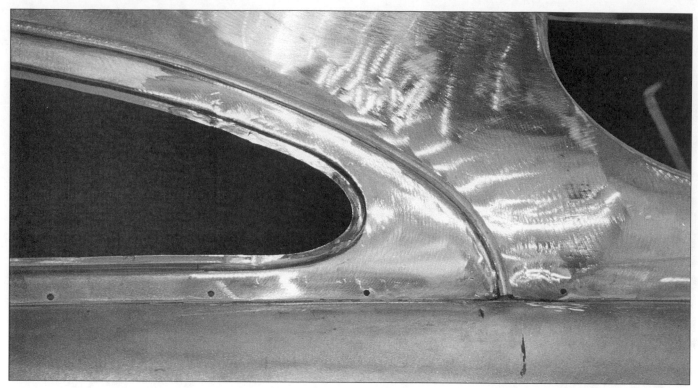

(courtesy of Kemps Rod and Restoration)

Once tacked, a small piece of flat metal is trimmed to fill in the gap behind the channel. Notice how the welds are almost impossible to detect after they have been ground flush.

(courtesy of Kemps Rod and Restoration)

The "B" pillar is angled forward to add detail to the body. The original posts were trimmed and stretched to fit the new angle. Once the posts have been welded in place, the body will be ready for body work. The greater the OEM angle of the front and rear windows, the more steps and work will be involved. This example represents one of the most elaborate and difficult chops you will encounter and costs around $15,000 if a professional does it for you.

(courtesy of Kemps Rod and Restoration)

Here is a '37 Chevy. The front and rear window frame on bodies of the late '30s have a moderate angle and are easier to work on.

(courtesy of Kemps Rod and Restoration)

The chop begins with the same referencing as the Merc. Since this will be a 2-inch chop, masking tape is used to mark off the cut lines and reference points can be seen on both sides of the front window frame as well as the rear quarter area.

(courtesy of Kemps Rod and Restoration)

The chop begins with the same referencing as the Merc. Since this will be a 2-inch chop, masking tape is used to mark off the cut lines and reference points can be seen on both sides of the front window frame as well as the rear quarter area.

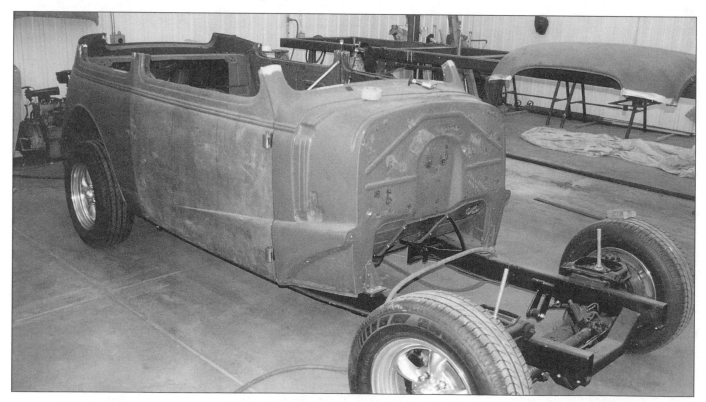

(courtesy of Kemps Rod and Restoration)

With any chop the body must be bolted to the frame, inner bracing added and thin cutoff wheels used to make the cuts.

The added brace from the door-jambs to the floor can be clearly seen. Since the rear window is almost perpendicular to the ground, the roof can be separated right through the center of the frame.

(courtesy of Kemps Rod and Restoration)

A similar support should be made for the roof as it is lined up to the "A" pillar.

(courtesy of Kemps Rod and Restoration)

Once the roof has lined up, check the gap at the rear of the car before welding.

(courtesy of Kemps Rod and Restoration)

In this case, the roof is too far forward, although not as severe as the Merc. This should happen on any body where the front and rear window frames are at an angle.

(courtesy of Kemps Rod and Restoration)

Instead of leaning the rear of the car farther forward, a cut can be placed across the top of the roof. This allows the rear portion of the roof to slide back and mate up with the body. However, it leaves about an inch-wide gap across the roof. A narrow strip of steel is trimmed and TIG welded to fill the gap. Every effort should be made to weld slowly and keep the metal cool as you weld. Notice how a small strip of steel is welded along the door channel. This acts as a straight edge to keep the roof in line.

(courtesy of Kemps Rod and Restoration)

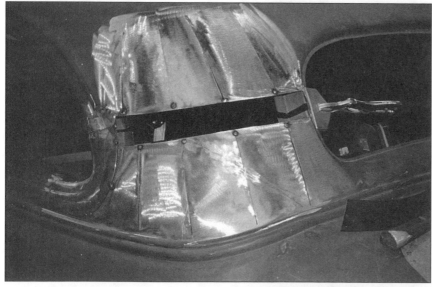

Even though the roof has been pulled back to mate the body, the new roof contour is not smooth and the curve at the bottom of the quarter glass needs to be changed. Vertical relief cuts are made and the metal is slightly bent to get the correct contour.

(courtesy of Kemps Rod and Restoration)

(courtesy of Kemps Rod and Restoration)

Even though the roof has been pulled back to mate the body, the new roof contour is not smooth and the curve at the bottom of the quarter glass needs to be changed. Vertical relief cuts are made and the metal is slightly bent to get the correct contour.

(courtesy of Kemps Rod and Restoration)

The bottom corner of the quarter glass frame is removed and reshaped to match the new contour.

The overall welding process is similar to the Merc in the sense that the welds start at the "A" pillar and move to the rear. The center roofstrip is welded next and the doors last. Your reference points should be checked repeatedly.

(courtesy of Kemps Rod and Restoration)

With the door frames welded in place, the overall chop is complete. This example has a moderate difficulty level and would cost around $8,000 in a shop.

(courtesy of Kemps Rod and Restoration)

The most classic of chops dates back to the early Fords. The Model A's front and rear window frames lie vertically. This greatly simplifies chop and lowers the cost of labor. Referencing and inner bracing is done first.

(courtesy of Kemps Rod and Restoration)

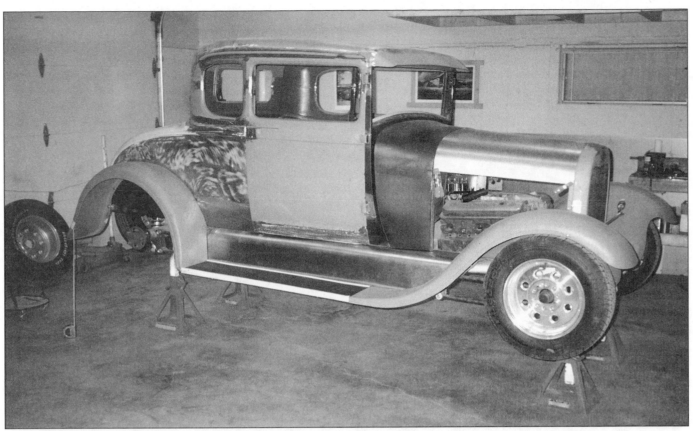

(courtesy of Kemps Rod and Restoration)

Model A chops are relatively simple and run about $4,000 in a shop. Here, a custom aluminum hood is also being manufactured. Notice how the body is being test fitted with the hood, fenders and running boards before any bodywork is done.

(courtesy of Kemps Rod and Restoration)

Custom fabricated hoods and hood inserts are very popular and add detail to the overall design. This '35 Plymouth has an aluminum hood that opens as one piece to the passenger side. The hood inserts on either side are also fabricated out of aluminum with custom stainless stripes.

(courtesy of Kemps Rod and Restoration)

(courtesy of Kemps Rod and Restoration)

A project like this starts with aluminum sheet stock. The two hood inserts are clamped together and cut out at the same time. Since the hood will be shaped, the aluminum sheet is annealed first to reduce brittleness and ease construction. To anneal aluminum, take an acetylene torch and blacken the metal with the oxygen turned off. Continue to heat the metal until the black stains burn off. This is the exact temperature that aluminum anneals and this process only has to be done once. Once cool, the metal will bend and shape easily without cracking.

(courtesy of Kemps Rod and Restoration)

The new hood is bent to the desired angle by hand. Looking down on the hood, the metal takes on a trapezoid shape. Experience is needed to know what angles to create, but the process can be simplified by making cardboard templates of the shape of the firewall and radiator shell. The shape is fine tuned with good old-ashioned trial and error as the hood is repeatedly checked against the body for the correct shape.

(courtesy of Kemps Rod and Restoration)

When the correct curve is achieved, the hood and inserts can be trimmed to fit.

(courtesy of Interiors by Shannon)

Frenching is a technique mostly used on brake and turn signal lights. Exterior bezels are removed and the lens is inserted flush to the panel. In this example, a threaded stud is welded on the back side of the fenders about 3/8 inch above and below the hole for the brake light lens. The plastic lens is cut so that it fits exactly flush inside the hole. A plastic lip or flange is glued to the back side of the lens and holes are drilled in the flange to match the studs on the inside of the panel. When the lens is inserted from the back side of the panel, flat washers and nylon lock nuts hold the entire light bulb housing and lens in place.

(courtesy of Street Rods by Michael)

Hidden door handles are very popular. A small transmitter, usually on a key chain, signals a solenoid to pop the door latch. It is important that door seals are not so thick that the door binds when latched. It is also recommended that the standard door latches be replaced with bear claw latches to ease release. Remote entry kits cost around $200 plus the labor to modify the door.

Chapter 8

Bodywork

A successful paint job starts with the quality of the bodywork. Paint is nothing more than a colored, mirror finish to bodywork. If dents are not repaired or the panels are wavy, the paint will only magnify the problem and make the mistakes easier to see.

Block sanding is the process of repeatedly sanding a panel to remove defects and it is this process that is the secret professionals use to get incredible looking paint. When you stand at the front of a hot rod and look down the length of the car, the surface should reflect a clear image of the surrounding area. If the panels have not been blocked properly, the reflection will be wavy and distorted.

In this chapter, we'll examine the techniques used in block sanding. Top-notch paint and body men get paid well for a reason. Blocking takes time, patience, physical effort and skill. The first step is understanding how the different chemicals, materials and tools are used.

TOOLS OF THE TRADE

Fortunately, the tools are not numerous or expensive. You will need an assortment of blocks, most of which you can make yourself. The sandpaper used in blocking is available through 3M and comes in a continuous roll. The paper is torn off to the length you need to match your block, but the width is always the same. The purpose of the block is to support the paper and keep it flat so you do not sand primer or body filler out of the low areas on the panel.

I frequently find myself making a new block every time I tackle a new project and over the years I have collected dozens of blocks. For example, a standard 12-inch or 18-inch flat block can be purchased from almost any automotive paint supplier. They are usually made out of plastic and have convenient handles to hold on to. These are a good start and I recommend purchasing them.

You may find yourself with an narrow, concave shape that needs blocking. The top of the quarter panels of a late '60's Camaro have such an odd shape that a flat board-like shape will not fit down in such a curve. A flat board will only touch the surface on the very edges of the block and actually cut little grooves or gouges on the panels. To solve the problem, I found myself making a block out of discarded rubber hose. Bingo, now you have another block in your collection.

In addition to blocks, you will need an air compressor and a primer gun. It is important to have filters on your air lines to eliminate condensation and oil out of any air that will be used to spray paint or primer. It is during this

This roof alone has more surface area than most Model As. Bodywork is a matter of time and materials. The larger the car, the more expensive the entire project will be.

As you block a panel, the surface will take on a tiger-striped appearance as high and low spots reveal themselves. Surfacer can be applied just in the low spots and blocked again to save time and material. Continue to block the darker areas until there are metal spots showing over the entire panel like this. Notice how curved metal areas, called "eyebrows," will show up on either side of a low spot.

phase that you first get exposed to the airborne chemicals and fumes that can cause health problems. It is important to isolate yourself from chemicals like primer and the best way to do this is to wear gloves, eye protection and a government approved air respirator.

I would recommend going even one step further if you intend to do your own bodywork and purchase a hooded suit and an outside air supply unit. The suit is not expensive, but the air unit costs around $1,000. This unit pumps fresh air into your suit and is the only way to fully isolate yourself from the harmful chemicals found in urethane primer.

Two tools that are not mandatory, but are great time savers are a dual-action sander (DA) and an air file sander. Both of these tools use air to drive a high-speed sanding surface. The DA has a 6- or 8-inch circular pad and the file sander has a straight 16-inch pad. Both cost around $200 and save time on all of the initial body work steps but get less useful as you begin to fine tune the panel.

Saw horses are useful when blocking, priming or painting removable panels like hoods, doors, fenders, etc. You can make them yourself out of wood with only a nominal investment. Some professionals use a more complicated saw horse called a body dolly or jig. These are made out of metal and vary in size from some small enough to hold a fender to others designed to hold and rotate an entire car. Even though they are useful, I would not encourage the investment unless you intend to paint many cars.

An assortment of blocks is needed in bodywork. Curved areas like this fender can't be blocked with flat boards. 3M makes foam hand pads for tight curves. Narrow, flexible boards can also be made with paint sticks.

(courtesy of TL Rod and Custom)

The best way to prime in low-air flow environments is to use a complete paint suit and hood with an outside air supply unit.

Most professionals use a gravity-fed primer gun. Downdraft spray booths cost between $50,000-$100,000 and are out of reach for most hobbyists. In a high-air flow area, standard respirators are frequently used, but you should use a complete paint suit and an outside air supply unit. Primers and paint have the same dangerous chemicals in them.

(courtesy of TL Rod and Custom)

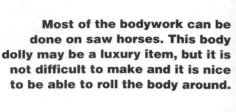

Most of the bodywork can be done on saw horses. This body dolly may be a luxury item, but it is not difficult to make and it is nice to be able to roll the body around.

There are a few terms you need to know to make sense of the different materials and their labels. The first is substrate; defined in a dictionary as "the material or substance on which an enzyme acts" or "an underlying layer." When paint companies use this word, what they really mean is "the surface you are about to apply something to and what it is made of." If you are spraying primer on an engine block, then the substrate is cast iron. The substrate on a fiberglass car body is not fiberglass, it is gel coat. If you sand through the gel coat then the substrate is both gel coat and fiberglass. Also, if the surface has been primed, then the substrate is the primer, not the metal underneath.

PRIMERS AND SURFACERS

There are two liquid chemicals used in bodywork: primer and surfacer. Primers are chemicals that adhere to the initial substrates: steel, iron, gel coat, aluminum, fiberglass, etc. Only enough primer to cover the substrate one time is needed to do the job. I will refer to this as one coat. That does not mean that you will spray one pass over the surface to create one coat. Primers are very thin and easy to run. You will need to spray them in light, see-through coats to prevent runs. You may need to make two or three thin passes over the substrate before one coat can be applied.

Surfacers are designed to be applied over primers. They are used to build material thickness for sanding and to provide a surface for paint to adhere to. Some paint companies offer products called primer/ surfacers. These are surfacers that have bonding characteristics like primer. What can be confusing is the paint manufacturers use the proper terms, but the professionals often call everything "primer." If you hire someone to do your bodywork, the term "primer" is loosely used and if you do your own bodywork, you need to be specific in what you ask for at the paint store. If you just ask for primer, there's no telling what you'll get.

(courtesy of Spies Hecker)

When you go to the paint store, it's best to keep your primers, sealers and surfacers all within one paint line. For example, using PPG primer, followed with Spies Hecker surfacer and Dupont paint is asking for major problems. "2K" on this label means that this primer/surfacer is mixed with a hardener to cure. The number 5110 is the actual product name and these change over the years. As long as you know the basic chemical and can describe what it does, the paint store will be able to help you.

Different primers are used depending on the substrate and stage of body work you're in. Self-etching or wash primers have acid in them that chemically bond with metal. Different wash primers are used depending on the metal. Etching primers are mandatory when working with aluminum. After the aluminum has been cleaned, a coat of alodyne is applied. Alodyne uses chromic acid to prep the metal for other primers. It is usually rubbed on by hand and the excess washed off with water. After the surface has dried, a coat of zinc chromate self-etching primer is applied and followed by epoxy.

Stainless steel uses a similar process, but skips the alodyne and starts off using zinc chromate followed by epoxy. I've tried applying straight epoxy to stainless, but it peels right off. Iron and steel work better with phosphoric acid. This acid has a unique quality that attacks rust very quickly, but is very mild on the rest of the metal. Steel-oriented wash primers generally use phosphoric acid as the reducer. This primer is not mandatory for steel or iron. It typically is used on metal that was not sand blasted or sanded with a dual-action sander. I recommend its use if the bare steel has been exposed to air longer than 24 hours after it has been stripped. This is a "just in case" measure to neutralize any oxidation that can't be seen with the naked eye.

None of these primers protect the surface from moisture for any length of time and they weaken or peel under heat. It is not recommended to use any kind of body filler over them as the heat produced during the curing process can damage the primer. If you choose to use wash primer, apply no more than a half coat and follow by applying a coat of epoxy primer before moving on to other steps.

Epoxy primers are useful because they do not react with acid-, lacquer- or enamel-based primers. They are chemically neutral so they are used to seal old paint, primer, bodywork or fiberglass. Epoxy is both heat and chip resistant so it is perfect for chassis components, radiators, engine blocks, inner fender wells or any other area that may take a lot of abuse. Epoxy is water resistant, so it provides good protection for parts that may sit for a while before paint. It does not hold up to extended sunlight exposure, so you cannot store the parts outside, but it will protect metal from condensation and humidity.

High build primer/surfacers are used to cover bodywork and fill in low spots during the block sanding process. High build primers are designed to be thick so they don't flow out of normal paint guns well. Most painters have at least three spray guns. Two of the guns use a 1.3mm tip. One gun is for sealers or single-stage paints and the other gun is used for clear coats only. This helps keep the clear coat clean and free of contaminants. The third gun is used for primer and uses a larger diameter tip. I've seen tips ranging between 1.8 and 2.3mm depending on the painter's personal preference. The larger the diameter, the more material will be applied with each pass.

Since all of the different primers touch each other, it is a good idea to use products from one paint line or manufacturer. Mixing different manufacturers, brands and lines is one of the most common reasons for paint failure amongst "do it yourself' paint and body men.

BODY FILLER

Polyester body filler has gotten a bad rap over the years. There are multiple brands and they are all very similar. Bondo is a highly recognized name brand and it seems that at every show, I hear people talking down about the product. Bondo has the same quality as any other polyester filler, but since it is sold in almost every auto parts store, people who know nothing about paint and bodywork have access to it and use it incorrectly. All polyester filler products are hygroscopic, meaning they absorb water. After these fillers are applied, they cannot be wet sanded or stored outside. The filler will absorb water and cause the steel underneath to rust. I have often stripped cars and found rust under body filler. This is why I recommend applying a coat of epoxy first to provide a barrier between the metal and filler. Most labels will tell you it's OK to apply filler over steel, but why take a chance?

Body filler can be found in two forms, a spreadable paste or a liquid that can be sprayed out of a primer gun. Both types have a hardener and it is important that the hardener get mixed into the filler thoroughly. If not mixed right, the filler can lift off of the surface later on. I can never say enough positive things about spray polyester. It is an incredible time saver. The blocking process is very repetitive because you continually apply primer over the panel and sand the material off. Spray polyester cuts multiple blocking cycles out of the project because its thickness fills in low spots better than ordinary primer.

Traditionally body filler was rough sanded with 40 grit or a file and finished by hand. This technique damages the surrounding area with deep scratches, so I recommend using a dual-action or power block sander with 80-grit paper to sand the filler close to flush and then finish sanding by hand in stages with 180-, 220- and 320-grit paper until the filler is smooth and the low spot can no longer be detected.

ONE STEP AT A TIME

Every painter is different, but I have a process I use that is the same for fiberglass and steel-bodied cars. Starting with the chassis, the components are sandblasted to remove rust, oil or paint. The surface is then blown off multiple times. Sandblasting cuts small pits into the steel that trap silica dust. One way to remove this dust is to wipe the entire surface with wax and grease remover and paper towels. However, wiping down an entire frame like this is time consuming. Scrubbing the metal with a Scotch Brite pad while blowing the surface with compressed air works just as well. One coat of epoxy primer is applied and allowed to cure. Any pits or stamping marks are covered with polyester filler and sanded flush.

One paint defect is called "edge mapping." This defect is caused when the body filler absorbs chemicals out of the primer and swells. The risk of edge mapping can be reduced by sanding body filler with finer grits and coating them with epoxy before any further primer coats are applied. On chassis parts, two coats of epoxy primer can be applied over the bodywork and inspected to see if the repair is finished. You may need to repeat the process if the area still looks damaged or a spot was missed. The epoxy can be wet sanded with 500 grit and prepped for paint.

If you are using a powder coat system on your chassis, you should not fill or prime the steel. Powder coat is applied over bare steel only.

OUTSIDE PANELS

Bodywork on the outside panels of the car is more involved. After the steel has been stripped of paint and rust, the panels should be sanded with a dual-action sander using 80-grit paper. Take note of any dented areas that need repair. Dents that have easy access on both sides of the metal are tapped out using a variety of body hammers. The other side of the metal is backed by a dolly to prevent the metal from being tapped too far, thus creating a high spot. There are a wide variety of hammers available, but every body man seems to have a favorite. I find myself grabbing for a pick hammer without even thinking about it. Slapping spoons are usually used to work high spots. The metal is still backed by a dolly, but the spoon slaps the metal smooth so it is flush with the surrounding area. Body files are used to find subtle dents and remove slight high spots.

Dents that do not have full access will need to be pulled. The traditional technique involved drilling holes in the low spots of the dent. A slide hammer screwed into the hole and tapped the dent out. The problem with this technique is that it left multiple holes which then had to be welded up. Spot-weld dent pullers were introduced to save time. With this technique small pins are welded to the low areas of the dents. The pins are

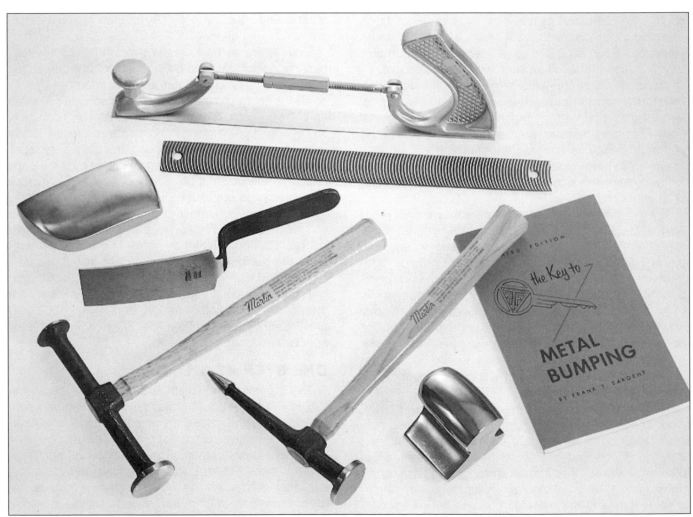

(courtesy of the Eastwood Company)

Starting at the top and working counterclockwise, body files are used to sculpt lead and to find high and low spots on panels before the blocking process. A slapping spoon and dolly are used on high spots. The dolly is placed on the back side of the metal as the spoon forces the high spots out and flush with the rest of the panel. Various shaped hammers work in similar ways depending on the shape of the dent.

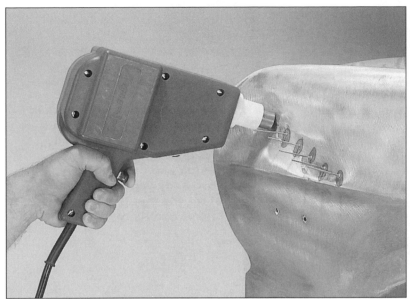

Spot weld dent pullers are ideal for dents that cannot be tapped out from the rear and cost around $300.

(courtesy of the Eastwood Company)

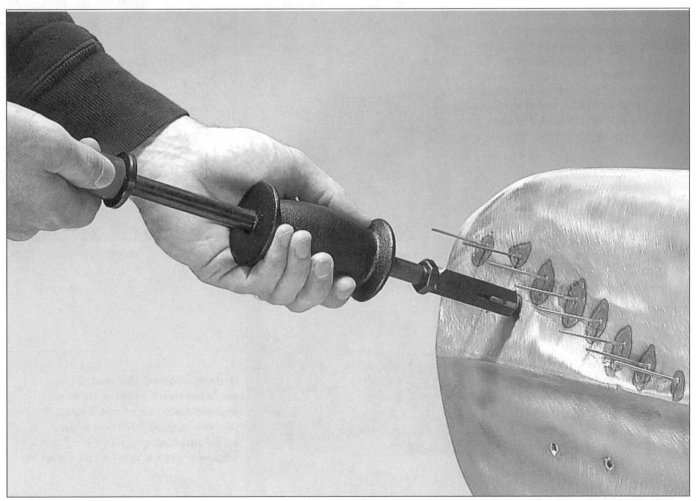

(courtesy of the Eastwood Company)

This dent puller comes with the kit. It holds the copper pin as you slide the weight back against the stop. The tapping motion hammers the dent out. Be careful not to get your hand caught between the base and the weight as you tap.

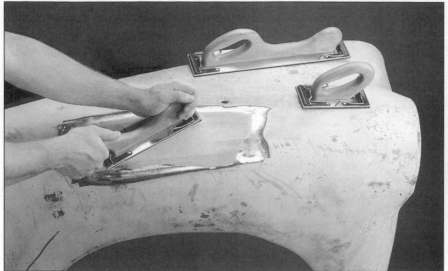

Initial dents are usually worked out on bare steel. I would add one thing to this photo. Body fillers absorb moisture and applying one coat of epoxy before bodywork will help protect the metal and provide a higher quality repair.

(courtesy of the Eastwood Company)

Small areas missed during the strip process can be cleaned up with an abbrasive disk before priming is done.

(courtesy of TL Rod and Custom)

Before primer, the metal should be bright and shinny. Rust pits should be ground out with a die grinder, reinforced areas sandblasted and exterior panels sanded with a dual-action sander.

(courtesy of Kemps Rod and Restoration)

The earliest hot rods came from stripped down Model T bodies. The roof, fenders and hood are all removed to reduce weight. Before World War II, these cars served as experimental speed machines and laid the foundation for the hot rod craze that would follow the war. Notice how the simple paint scheme and original-style wheels give this car a nostalgic, almost "time-warped" appearance. Selecting your car's theme is the most important decision you will make throughout the project.

Another look at a traditional hot rod. This theme has been kept very simple. Model As are the most affordable hot rod to build as they have few parts and a simple design. A car like this can be built for $17,000 or less, depending on how much work you do yourself.

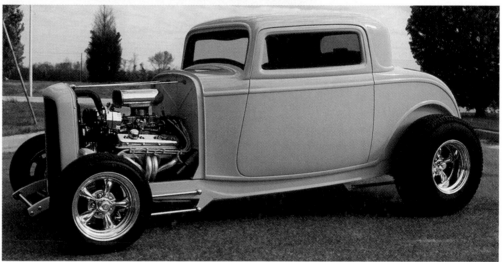

This traditional hot rod, a 1933 Viper sedan owned by Bill McQueen, has several additions that would add points in a show. Most of the chassis components have been chrome plated. Precision stitched upholstery and a high end (high horsepower) engine all add detail to the project. Added details are essential for show cars. Expect a car like this to run between $50,000 and $80,000, depending on chrome and extra detail.

McQueen's simple, classy interior.

Model T panel wagons are fairly rare. Few were built and most were scrapped as they were considered "junked" work trucks. These cars always turn heads. After all, how many boys had a toy Matchbox or Hot Wheel car that looked liked this?

Modified Model As are some of the most traditional hot rods. After World War II, hot rodders had an almost endless supply of cheap cars and parts to tinker with.

Made popular by television, movies and music videos, early '30s Fords stand out as the premier example of what a street rod is all about. In fact, most clubs classify a street rod as any pre-1949 custom car.

Changing the original function or shape of a factory panel takes advanced building skill. Not only does this hood open forward, but it opens with both front fenders attached as well. Expect a modification like this to add several thousand dollars to your expense sheet.

The terms "hot rod" and "street rod" are frequently used to describe the same thing and are often interchangeable. Many people refer to Ford Model Ts and As as hot rods and all other cars up through 1948 as street rods. Cars from the late '30s and early '40s are almost always referred to as street rods and are usually built with their sheet metal intact, like the hood, fenders and step panels.

This traditional custom theme boasts yellow flames over black paint. The darker the color, the more precise the bodywork has to be. Dark colors magnify flaws like dents and wavy bodywork where light colors have a tendency to hide them.

Even though the car body is similar, a different effect is achieved by using non-traditional colors and a more futuristic grille. Interlacing the tips of the flames will give you a more fluid and artistic design.

This car is a replica of the famous Hirohata Merc built by Stan Barris. The seafoam and organic green 1951 Mercury was widely copied. Notice how the side window frames are curved and the grille has been heavily modified. The radical bodywork has been offset with a traditional color, wheels and white walls. There is no real right and wrong in custom cars.

This Ford is lightly modified. The paint, grille and turn signals have been changed, but otherwise this is a stock car. The fewer the modifications, the more affordable the project will be.

It's not hard to run up $12,000 when you put together a nice engine like this. The blower on this flathead engine is cool, but it also adds to the cost.

Ladder bars are good for cars meant to go fast, but aren't recommended for street cruising.

The contrast of color, chrome and aluminum can look great on the front end of a car and under the hood. Such detail doesn't come cheaply, however.

This car may have started out as a '40 Ford, but it has been transformed into a totally new creation.

This car is a trick. It looks like a Model A hot rod but is really a '98 Lexus shown at the Chicago Auto Show. Hot rodding is having a greater impact on production cars each year.

Kyle Bond's five-window Gibbon's Viper II.

A Gibbon body "flathead flyer."

Jay Lewis's hot 1934 Viper coupe.

Jerry Uttrachi's silver 1934 Tudor.

Ron Zimmerman's 1932 Cabriolet pickup with windows.

Kyle Bond's radical '33 Ford alcohol dragster.

Power packed: Bond's dragster has clocked 8.59 seconds at 168 mph in the quarter mile.

Paul and Bonnie Katzke's 1946 Chevy truck.

placed every 3/4 of an inch or so. A special slide hammer is used to grab the pin and tap the dent out. When the dent is pulled the pin is cut off and ground flush with the rest of the panel. Spot-weld dent pullers cost around $300 for a complete kit.

After the dents are pulled, the entire car panel should be rubbed with a Scotch Brite pad and blown with compressed air like the chassis was. Sandblasting leaves sand and dust in the cracks or joints of the body, so blow the car off repeatedly until no more sand is seen falling off the body. The outside panels should be wiped with wax and grease remover as an additional step. One coat of epoxy primer is applied to the entire body and allowed to cure. Polyester body filler is then applied over the dented areas and sanded flush with a block or dual action sander in stages with 80-, 120-, 220- and 320-grit paper.

You may want to explore the lost art of leading dents or low spots. Leading is fun, but isn't very practical. Extra care has been given throughout the project to ensure that the panels are not exposed to heat. You take a big chance in warping the panels during the leading process. Molten lead is too hot to be applied over primer, so it cannot be used during the block stage.You are probably familiar with the health risks associated with lead poisoning. I do not feel comfortable encouraging anybody to do something that leaves powdered lead in the environment.

The entire body should be blown off again and the sanded body filler cleaned with wax and grease remover. Epoxy is used to seal the sanded body filler and prevent edge mapping problems. Two to four coats of high build surfacer or spray polyester is applied over the epoxy with repeated coats applied to areas you intend to block sand, like the fenders, quarter panels, hood, etc. How do you know when to use high build primers as opposed to spray polyesters? Spray polyesters build up thick and are great time savers during the blocking process. I usually use spray polyester on the exterior panels for two to three blocking cycles or until I see that the panels are getting straight. Once the panels no longer show any obvious high or low spots, I switch to urethane surfacer and start using a finer sanding grit like 180- or 240-grit paper. The purpose of shifting to finer grits as you fine tune the panels, is to reduce the chance of any sanding scratches showing themselves under the paint as the chemicals cure and slightly shrink over several weeks. High build products usually go on heavy and some practice is needed to see how heavy the surfacer can be applied before it runs. One pass over the surface usually applies several coats at a time. Six to eight coats (not passes) are applied to the panels. Once cured, these panels are ready to be blocked.

BLOCKING

The sides of your car are not smooth. They look more like the waves of an ocean with subtle high and low places. Blocking is the process of leveling these high and low spots so there is a uniform surface. Start by placing a thin guide coat over the surfacer to be blocked. The guide coat will be used to measure where you are sanding sur-

High-quality bodywork should be straight and dent free. To test this, sight down the length of the body and look at the reflection in the surface. Incorrect bodywork will produce a reflection that is distorted or flutters when you move.

The horizontal stripes seen on the door and fender are applied with a spray can. This is the traditional method for applying guide coat. 3M makes a dry-powdered guide coat that is easy to use. Try both and see which one works best for you.

(courtesy of Kemps Rod and Restoration)

Initial block sanding has shown a large low spot just beneath the block. This block was made out of balsa wood.

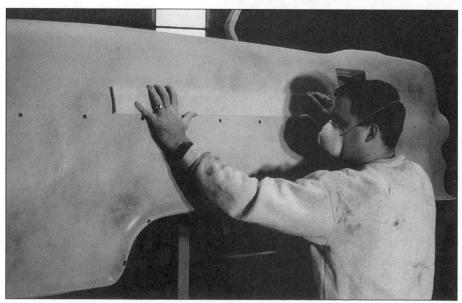

The longest block needed for sanding would be about 3 feet. This is necessary on most cars starting in the late 1940s through the '50s. The longer the car, the more difficult the blocking process is. Take this into consideration as you plan your budget.

The lines on the side of this building make a perfect background to check bodywork. Primer has no gloss, but you can wipe the surface with wax and grease remover to produce a temporary reflection.

facer off and where you are not. The places where the guide coat comes off quickly are the high spots and the places where the guide coat is untouched are the low spots. A common guide coat technique is to mist spray paint over the surfacer. However, when sanded, the paint has a tendency to gum up on the sandpaper. 3M makes a dry-powdered guide coat that works better. The powder is smeared over the surface with a foam applicator. There is no wait time. The surface is ready to be block sanded as soon as the guide coat is applied.

If you were to take a piece of sandpaper in your hand and start sanding the guide coat, you effectively accomplish nothing. You hand flexes with the contour of the low spots so you would sand surfacer out of the low spots as well as off the high ones. The panel would look the same. Block sanding uses file sandpaper backed by a firm board to keep the paper flat. When sanding with a block, the surfacer is sanded off of the high area without touching the low spots. This is good, because you want the low areas to get filled in without excessive material buildup. A low spot might be a foot wide or more, so the length of the sanding board is important. The board or block should be about half the length of the panel to be effective. If you are blocking a door that is 2 feet long then the block should be around a foot long. Most hot rods have short panels as the cars of the '30s weren't very long, but as you move into the '50s and '60s, cars get upwards of 18 feet in length or more. Some quarter panels are at least 6 feet long, so an ideal block would be 3 feet long. File sandpaper is purchased in rolls so any length can be used.

After selecting a block, sand the surfacer with 120-grit paper at 45-degree angles from left to right several strokes and then switch and sand the other direction. Try not to press too hard against the panel as you do not want it to flex during the process. Constantly move around the panel so you are sanding around the panel

equally. As you are sanding, watch the guide coat on the surface and take note of any places where metal shows up immediately. These areas are the high spots that will need to be lightly tapped with a pick hammer. Continue to block the panel until metal spots are showing in several places on the panel. The panel should be cleaned again in preparation for the next coats of surfacer.

Your next step is somewhat of a judgment call because there are different ways to handle low spots depending on how deep they are. Place a straight edge over the low spot. If the area is more than 3/16 inch deep, then the area should be treated as a dent. Panels that can be accessed from the back side can be tapped out or a dent puller used to work the dent out. For spots where the metal is close to 3/16 inch deep, body filler can be used to fill in the low spots. Most of the areas will not be that deep, though.

For the rest of the low spots, you can either apply more coats of high build surfacer or spray polyester filler. When you just spray material in localized areas it is called "spotting." Both of these chemicals can be spotted in the low spots. Block sand your body filler and spotted areas and clean the area again. The panels are sprayed again with six to eight coats of high build surfacer and the whole blocking process is repeated. There is no need to add more material to the structural areas like the jams or firewall — just the exterior panels. If your blocking was done correctly, the high spots should take longer to show up and the low spots should all be shallow. High build primer can be spotted in the low spots and the entire process is repeated.

As you work through the blocking steps, the low areas should get smaller and smaller. You can test to see if a panel is finished by wiping the panel with wax and grease remover and looking at an image in the reflection. As you move your head from side to side, the image should stay steady and look smooth. If it is distorted or flutters, then the panel needs further blocking.

There will be several places where a traditional block cannot be used. You may need to fabricate custom blocks out of balsa wood or foam to address narrow areas or curved places around the edges of the body. A wide assortment of lengths and shapes will be used throughout the blocking phase. When it appears that the panel is close to being finished, switch to a less aggressive grit such as 220. Finish blocking the panels using 320-grit paper and double check the panel for straightness using wax and grease remover. You may find yourself going through six blocking sessions or more depending on the length of the vehicle.

When your bodywork is finished, lightly sand any overspray off the entire vehicle with 320 grit and wet sand the entire body with both 400- and 600-grit wet sanding paper. No bare metal spots should be showing. If you sand through the surfacer, spot in more surfacer or epoxy primer and wet sand your spotted areas again. The entire vehicle should be cleaned at least two times before moving on to paint.

QUALITY CONTROL IS THE CUSTOMER'S JOB

Bodywork is the most important step to a high-quality paint job. Not all professionals know how to do it right, either. All the word "professional" means is that a person does the work as their primary means of support. It doesn't mean that the individual has the necessary skill. To give you an example of how bad professional body work can get, I'll share a story about a '58 Chevy I worked on a few years back.

This particular car was brought to the shop because the previous shop and the owner had a falling out. This is not uncommon in the industry, so I wasn't suspicious of a problem right off the bat. The car body was painted, buffed and sitting on the chassis. All we needed to do was the final assembly work and the customer agreed to our standard hourly rate. He had already spent $25,000 for rust repair, bodywork and paint and I guessed we would need another $10,000 plus parts to finish the job. At first glance, the paint looked alright to me. It was buffed out nicely and the bodywork was close to straight so the job didn't seem like it would be that big of a deal, but I honestly didn't sit down and pick over the car or check the panels with a magnet.

When it comes time to line up and install the stainless trim, I like to see how well the pieces fit to the car and line up. This is where the first problem popped up. None of the quarter panel trim would fit the car. Naturally, I assumed there was a problem with the trim, but these parts were in excellent shape. It was like they were for a different car because the curvature between the panels and the trim was completely wrong.

I stopped and just studied the car for a second and something else looked strange. A '58 Chevy Impala has little racing scoops stamped into the sheet metal just behind the door and this car didn't have those on either side. Up until this point, I had never seen really bad bodywork before, so my first thought was that we had some factory mistake and that we may have a very rare car on our hands. I briefly got excited!

So I looked inside the car through the hole that would contain the rear quarter glass and the stamping was visible on the inside of the panel. "What the ... ? How is this possible?" Then I noticed something else. In this same area, there is a triangular brace that holds the convertible top piston to the floor. I could see where the brace was, but it had been cut away from the floor. This also baffled me, because why would anybody of sound mind destroy or remove anything that has to do with the top mechanism? I decided to just stop and examine the car from head to toe.

After extensive study of the car, both inside and out, the mystery unraveled. This car had had extensive rust problems. Most of the floor was rusted away like Swiss cheese and covered with filler, the body mounts were gone and covered over, and the perimeter of the body had plates brazed over rust and covered over with slabs of body filler. There was no real metal supporting the portion of the floor that holds the front seat. The customer could have gotten out on the highway and become intimate with the road if you know what I mean. This car was a complete disaster! There were places where the body filler was over an inch thick. As the foreman, I had the unpleasant task of educating the customer that all of his $25,000 was wasted.

He then had to pay us to strip the car down to bare metal and start over again. At each step we would find some new disaster or challenge to overcome. I have never seen work this bad in my entire career. The customer stayed with us through the rust repair phase and through the point where the rear portion of the body got painted. However, by this time he had more than $50,000 spent and very little to show for it. He ran out of money and had to sell the car at a huge loss.

I never had the heart to ask him what he got for the car, but I would guess he got less than $20,000 for it. I lost track of him over the years, but I heard the project damaged his marriage.

It's a sad story, but two very important lessons can be learned from this. First, it is your responsibility to verify the level of competency of the people you hire to work on your car. You are essentially a project manager and are no different from a foreman supervising the building of a bridge. If the bridge falls, management gets blamed and the individual workers disappear. What control will you have over the process? You need to make monthly visits and inspect all of the work as it is being done. Insist on daily or weekly photo documentation.

Second, you should see finished products or examples of the shop's work and talk to former customers before making any decisions. Incompetent people burn lots of bridges. Lastly, avoid and be suspicious of any requests for large deposits. Struggling shops will take in more work than they can accomplish to get the deposits to pay bills. Sooner or later the house of cards caves in.

Chapter 9

Paint

The field of automotive paint is surrounded in myth, mystery and misinformation. Car shows and swap meets are full of people giving advice who have never sprayed a drop of paint in their lives. Paint is the one area where advice should be taken from professionals only. A lot of people encourage hobbyists not to do their own paint work.

Obviously, painting takes skill. Professional painters at high-volume collision centers are well paid and for good reason. The skills they possess take time to learn and their jobs are difficult. Most of these skills are learned the old-fashioned way — through trial and error. We learn by making mistakes, but painting mistakes are time consuming and expensive to fix. If a mistake requires repainting, a day is needed for the paint to dry, and then time is needed to sand the area smooth again. Professionals count all of the time needed to do this and many shops do not pay their employees for redo work. The material expense is also measured. A gallon of paint can run upwards of $500, so numerous mistakes can rapidly eat any savings you may have had by doing the work yourself.

To limit rework expenses, I like to start new painters out on small parts like chassis or engine compartment components. The smaller parts use less material and take less time to repair should a mistake be made. As your skills improve, you can move on to panels, like a door or fender. It may take several years to acquire enough skill to tackle a complete body, so patience is critical.

Modern paints are toxic and can propose a serious health risk if handled improperly — another reason why knowledge and experience are important. The paint needs to be sprayed in a clean, well-ventilated area. These concepts don't mix well because the faster you move the air in your painting environment, the more dust or contaminant gets stirred up and settles in your paint. In addition to air flow, safety equipment is needed to isolate you from the chemicals and this equipment can get pricey. New safety equipment can cost more than the initial paint job. The purchase is really only justified if you intend to paint several cars as an ongoing hobby.

High-quality paint work is expensive. If you opt to have a professional do both your paint and bodywork, you should expect bids between $6,000 and $20,000 to paint a car, depending on the quality of the finish and the size of the vehicle. If you do the bodywork yourself, you can cut these figures in half. Expensive? After you read this chapter and see what's involved, you may not think so.

PAINT HISTORY

Lacquer paint has been in use for more than 600 years. It was used to finish furniture and temples as far back as 1397 in Asia. However, it wasn't until the turn of the 20th century that it became practical in industrial applications. Ford really refined the formula and made it practical.

Lacquer dries very quickly and refinishers love it because it is easy to use and doesn't require expensive equipment to apply. When lacquer is sprayed, it lays down smooth, but doesn't dry glossy. Both manufactur-

(courtesy of the Eastwood Company)

Urethane paint is highly toxic. Gloves, paint suits and an outside air supply are required to protect you from the chemicals.

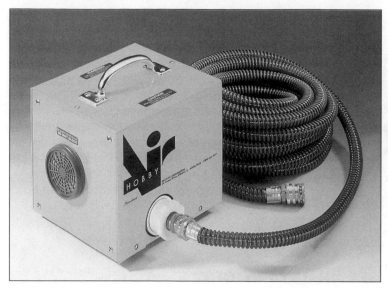

Outside air supply kits cost around $600. If you choose to do the painting yourself, please factor the necessary safety equipment into your budget.

(courtesy of the Eastwood Company)

ers and refinishers have had to polish the paint to get it to shine. This process is slow and expensive, especially in an assembly line atmosphere.

Manufacturers sought ways to eliminate the polishing step and eventually introduced enamel paints that dry glossy, thus eliminating the manual polishing step. Refinishers and hot rodders resisted this paint through the '70s because enamels dry slowly and with a bumpy texture called "orange peel." Put a polished lacquer finish next to an unpolished enamel one and the lacquer would win the show every time. Enamels could compete only if you sanded the orange peel off and polished the surface like you do with lacquer. Since lacquer dries almost orange peel free, the entire enamel process takes longer, so why bother? Both paints deteriorate about the same when exposed to the sun.

In the late '70s, urethane enamel became popular because it dries almost as quickly as lacquer, is more durable than either paint, and has more depth to its shine. The drawback is that the catalyst in urethane paint is derived from cyanide and is highly toxic. Not knowing better, over the years many of the "old timers" continued to spray the paint using the same dust masks they used with lacquer. This proved to be dangerous and accelerated retirement for many of them.

Urethane eventually became the new standard, but not for application reasons. It has a low VOC (volatile organic compound) content. VOCs have been linked to air pollution and are closely monitored by the government. Lacquer has a high VOC content. Even if you wanted to use lacquer, chances are you wouldn't be able to find it because it is restricted and regulated in most states. Urethane is the most common paint used in collision repair shops around the United States.

PAINT BASICS

Paint is composed of four parts: pigment, hardener, binder and reducer. The pigment is the color

that you actually see. Pigment is mixed into a clear binder, which is the liquid that makes up the majority of the paint. A hardener is added to the binder to create a reaction that cures the paint, and reducers are used to get the right viscosity so the paint sprays well. The reducers are the main source of VOCs, so paint companies have been trying to reduce or eliminate their use. The most common way this is done is to use paints with a high solid content and special guns that can lay the thicker paint down with minimal reducer content. These guns are called HVLP (high volume/low pressure) and can be purchased for around $400. They shoot high solid paint well by breaking the paint spray into a finer mist than traditional guns and are designed to spray at 25 to 35 lbs. of air pressure compared to the 45 to 55 lbs. normally used. The lower air pressure reduces overspray and waste. Most auto refinishers are using high solid paint with HVLP guns.

Another way to reduce VOCs is to use waterborne paint. Waterborne paints use distilled water as a reducer and special hardeners to chemically bond the paint in a way that is similar to normal urethanes. VOC content is greatly reduced, but this type of paint is difficult to use and requires special equipment to spray. If you live in a state that requires its use, and everything else is outlawed, it's best to take your car to a professional (or another state!). It just won't be practical to paint the car yourself.

PAINT STYLES

Any paint technology can then be divided into three more subgroups or styles: single stage, base coat/clear coat and pearl coat. The style is mostly determined by the color you choose and it is important to understand these terms (styles) so you can order paint properly. Each of these requires slightly different application techniques.

Solid colors — ones without metallic flake — are usually applied as a single-stage paint, which means

HVLP guns are specially designed for today's urethane paints. They lay paint down with less orange peel while conserving material at the same time.

(courtesy of the Eastwood Company)

that the pigment, binder, hardener and reducer are poured into one can, mixed and sprayed in one step. Red, yellow, white and black are all common single stage colors. The advantage to single stage paints is that they are applied as one spraying step, which reduces the amount of time for airborne contaminants to settle down in the paint. If you intend to paint the car yourself and do not have a paint booth, you may want to pick a solid color to reduce contaminants in your paint (there's that planning thing again.).

Two-stage or base coat/clear coat paint is applied in two spraying steps. The color is applied first in thin coats (called the base coat) and then followed with clear coats. The base coat dries quickly and is designed to allow the metal flake to lay flat against the car. The clear coats have the hardener and provide all the protective and durable qualities. A cleaner painting environment is needed because the application process takes longer with base coat/clear coat colors. Silver and gold are good examples of metallic paints that require paint to be sprayed in two steps.

Have you ever looked at a car and noticed that it changes colors depending on the angle you view it? This is called a pearl coat and it is applied in three steps. If you wanted a green car to shift to blue in the sun, then you would first apply a green ground coat. Then a special see-through pearl blue coat is applied followed by traditional clear. Pearl colors are difficult to spray.

Auto paint stores and most paint shops have volumes of paint chip books for you to thumb through to assist in color selection. It is expensive to change the color later on so take some time and make sure you have a color you like.

POWDER COATING

After the bodywork is finished, the body and frame can be separated. The painting process usually starts with the chassis, but the builder must decide if normal paint or powder coat will be used. Powder coating is essentially a dry paint process. The pieces are electrically charged and a powdered paint is fogged over the steel. The excess powder falls to the floor and is reused. After the parts are coated they are baked in an oven at 400 degrees to cure the paint. Powder coating dries glossy, gives off low emissions because there are no liquid solvents, is chip resistant and does not peal when exposed to brake fluid.

You can get just about any color you want and you can buy do-it-yourself kits for less than $300. The kit comes with everything needed to coat parts small enough to fit in your oven. There is really no practical way to apply powder coat to the body of the car, but many rodders prefer it on chassis components because it is so durable. You could mix the application, too. For example, you could paint the frame and powder coat the smaller parts. Some people like to take the large parts to a professional and purchase some of their powder to use at home for everything else.

Powder coating has many advantages, but it cannot be used on rubber or plastic. Some control arms or leaf springs have rubber bushings and they will not hold up to 400-degree temperatures. This heat issue could affect your entire plan. For example, the chassis must be fully assembled to do your bodywork and some parts require bushings. Bushings are not fun to install and they are even more difficult to remove, so you may need to powder coat some of your parts before you assemble the chassis. These parts will need special

(courtesy of Interiors by Shannon)

Part of your painting strategy is selecting the color itself. Lighter colors hide imperfections in bodywork and paint. If it is your intent to do all the work yourself you can use this trick to hide places of "learning."

(courtesy of Street Rods by Michael)

Most professionals disassemble the chassis before painting. This step is necessary if you choose to powder coat your components or if you are building a show car. If you are painting, you can save time by masking off places you don't want to paint and spraying the entire chassis assembly.

Professionals use jigs to paint or powder coat their frames. Although handy, they cost around $3,500.

attention throughout the project to avoid over spray and damage. Also, you cannot use any type of body filler with powder-coated paint. Let's say your frame has all kinds of pits and hammer marks in the steel. If you use traditional paint, you can prime the frame and use body filler to smooth out the rough spots. With a couple more coats of primer, the steel will look new again. There is no practical work-around for this process in powder coating yet. Conventional paint has fewer planning issues to consider and may be the best choice for first-time builders.

SAFETY

Urethane paint is not as easy to use as lacquer, but it can be applied by hobbyists. For health reasons, it requires the purchase of extra equipment to protect you from the chemicals. Gloves, goggles, paint suit and an outside air supply mask or respirator are required to isolate the painter from the toxins in the paint. This equipment costs between $1,000 and $2,000.

I've see many outstanding paint jobs that were sprayed in garages. Keep in mind that sufficient airflow is needed to pull the overspray and fumes out and away from both you and the car. Most hobbyists will line their garages with clear plastic, wet the floor and use a box fan to pull the fumes out. The toxins are not the only hazard, however. All paints form a flammable mist when sprayed, so the fan absolutely must be an explosion-proof fan. These types of fans are sealed so the fumes do not come in contact with the motor.

Lastly, I think it is important not to paint alone. I know of a guy, who was not using a proper respirator, who passed out in the booth. Since the booth had no windows, he was on the floor quite a while before anybody found him.

PAINTING PREP

Preparation is the key to good paint work. Before you begin, be sure to check the paint company's recommended preparation process. There are primers, surfacers and sealers. Some chemicals act as both. Technically, you can apply paint to any surfacer, but some brands insist on a sealer coat between the paint and the surfacer. This always makes me a little nervous because what they are indirectly telling you is that their paint line has inconsistencies so they need a barrier between their own chemicals. I avoid using brands like this.

Sealers have their place, however. During the sanding process, if you sanded through the surfacer and into old paint or primer, or if you are not using a primer that specifically says it is also a surfacer, then sealer is a good idea. If you sanded into some body-work, then paint will usually show rings on the feathered edges of primer or body filler. This is called "bulls eyeing." Sealers are used to prevent this as well. A normal paint color will completely cover in three coats, but if you find you need more, then apply a coat of tintable sealer between the surfacer and base coat. Tintable sealers allow you to mix in some base coat with the sealer to die it close to the final color, and this saves time and material.

When you feel your bodywork is finished and the surface is ready for paint, it is important that the surface is free of any heavy-grit sanding scratches. To remove these, first clean the surface with wax and grease remover the same way you cleaned during the body-work phase. Apply a light guide coat and block the surface with 240-grit dry sanding paper. If you break through the surfacer in several places, you will need to reapply surfacer and block with 240 again. When the panel is truly straight, you should be able to block with 240 without numerous or large break-through spots. Clean and lightly guide coat the surface again.

Every paint company is different, but usually the surface needs to be sanded with 400- to 600-grit wet sandpaper or 600-to 800-grit dry sanding paper. I prefer to 500-grit wet sand. This process eliminates dirt nubs or orange peel in the surfacer as well as the previous 240-grit scratches. Wet sand the area until all of the guide coat is gone. Both hard and soft wet-sanding blocks can be used, depending on the contour of the panel. The surface should then be wiped down with wax and grease remover until your paper towel looks clean. This usually takes two times. Blow off the surface with compressed air and lightly wipe with a tack cloth at least two times. It is important to spend extra time blowing in any area that might still have water left over from sanding. If your environment is clean and well ventilated, you are ready for the next step.

You may have some items you would like to mask off. Typical areas might be rubber gaskets on the chassis or different-colored areas on the dash. Be sure to use both paper and tape that are designed for automotive refinishing. Some tapes have a resin that reacts with paint. Masking off a design like flames, stripes or scallops comes later. You mask off anything you do not want paint on only at this time. If you touched the surface, then you will need to clean the surface again to remove any oils that may have come from your skin.

Normally, a coat of sealer is needed, so when the surface is clean, I like to blow the area off again and apply one coat of sealer. Sealers are designed to have paint sprayed right over the top of them without being sanded. This is called "wet on wet" or "non-sandable" sealer. You have a time window in which the paint must be applied

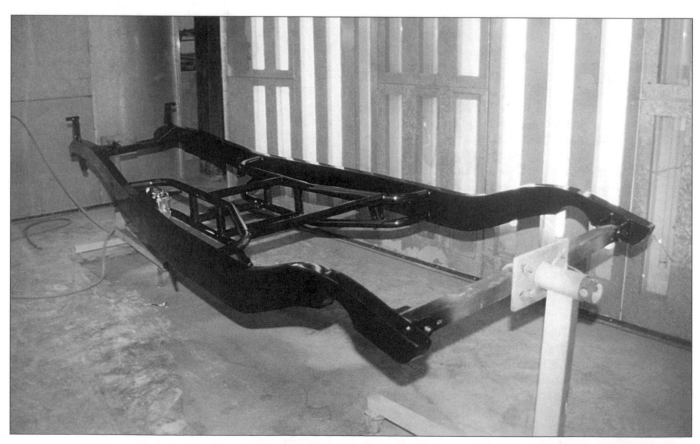

(courtesy of Gibbon Fiberglass Reproductions)

Using an engine stand at either end of the frame is an inexpensive way to build a frame jig. Engine stands can be found for around $300 each.

An even more affordable solution can be done with saw horses. Frames can be painted top side first, allowed to dry and flipped over so the saw horses rest on areas covered by the body. The overspray is almost impossible to detect.

and that is usually no longer than eight hours. Any longer and you will have to sand the sealer and apply a new coat. Sealers are usually much thinner than the primers you used during bodywork, so spray them in light coats. I often refer to a light coat as a half coat. One coat should just be enough to completely cover the surface, so a half coat should be see-through. Only one complete coat of sealer is needed to do the job, but you will reduce or eliminate runs if this coat is applied in half or even third coats, depending on how thin it is. Also, if you apply sealer in thin coats you will reduce orange peel that will be visible on the surface.

PAINT APPLICATION

As soon as the sealer has had enough time to flash off, the paint can be sprayed. Be sure to check the manufacturer labels for specific product information, because flash times differ between companies. Single-stage and two-stage paints are applied differently. The base coats are applied in thin half coats much like sealer until all of the sealer has been covered. Then apply two more half coats just to be safe because it is easy to miss spots when wearing a full paint suit and helmet. This should ensure proper coverage. You may see some trash or

dust in the paint. These will sand out of the top coats, but if the trash looks large, allow the base coat to dry (about 20 to 30 minutes) and lightly sand the contaminant out before applying the clear coat. If the contaminant is too large, you will sand through the clear coat during the color sanding phase. To avoid this, lightly sand the particles with 1,000-grit, clean and spray with base coat in those areas again. The base coat has a similar time window to the sealer (usually 8 hours or less) and must have the clear coat applied wet on wet.

Clear coats and single-stage top coats are applied much the same way. First, a half coat is applied to give the paint something to adhere to. Most painters call this a tack coat. After this coat has flashed off, a full coat can be applied. Repeat this process until a good three coats have been applied to the surface. Remember that these are wet, heavy coats so it will be easy to get runs. It is important to learn your paint brand's characteristics before painting any large areas. You may find that a 15-minute flash time is needed with some brands between every coat to avoid runs. Other brands will have the opposite problem in the sense that they may not run, but they are difficult to apply wet and glossy.

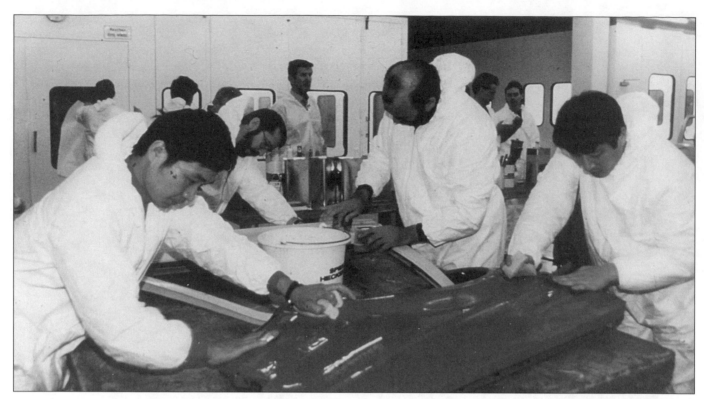

(courtesy of Spies Hecker, Inc.)

Most paint manufacturers offer weekend paint classes to teach new customers how to use their paint. The classes are inexpensive and are a must for new painters.

Experience will tell you if more coats are needed on the panels of the car because a few coats are removed during the color sanding and compounding process. Five to six coats may need to be applied to the exterior of the car or anything else you intend to polish. Urethane is a thick paint, unlike lacquer, so all that talk about applying 20 coats is lingo left over from the lacquer days.

There is a section in the back of this book that talks about paint failures. Solvent pop is a failure created by applying too much paint. Every paint is different, but three coats is a good average. You may need to spray the paint in heavier coats to get the paint to lay out the way you want it, in which case you may shoot two coats at a time. This requires trial and error to get right. You'll soon respect why good painters are hard to come by.

A bright, well-ventilated area is needed to paint. With some creativity, a homemade booth can be assembled in your garage using sheet plastic, an explosion proof box fan and conventional booth filters.

Sealer is not used to finish bodywork. Most sealers are designed to place a barrier between the primers and paint or to tint the surface so less paint is needed to cover properly.

Don't expect to paint like a professional right out of the gate. Painting chassis parts first will give you a chance to learn the characteristics of the paint before the large pieces are tackled.

You will need to experiment with your gun to understand how it sprays paint, but most painters spray with a full spraying pattern and hold the gun about 12 to 16 inches from the surface. Most paint companies offer a painting class to teach newcomers how to use their brand. A class like this is priceless!

SPECIAL EFFECTS

Flames, scallops and graphics require additional skills that can take as much time to perfect as painting itself. Beginners should consider planning a simple paint scheme for their first project or enlist the help of a professional. If you want to learn, there are a few tricks that will help you get a more professional-looking finish.

Professionals spray the primary color and entire design in base coat first and then clear over the surface last. This greatly reduces the rough edges that tape lines can cause. 3M makes a blue fine-line tape that provides a finer edge than traditional masking tape.

Using flames as an example, the surface is first sprayed the primary color (usually black). Once the base coat has thoroughly dried for at least 2 hours, the flame pattern is taped off using 1/8-inch fine-line tape. The rest of the surface is masked off using paper and normal masking tape. The surface is repeatedly checked to see if any fine-line tape is lifting off and the flame area is tacked off before the flames are sprayed. It is important

to keep the entire surface clean during the masking process because some base coats react with wax and grease remover. Although it's awkward at times, I like to wear rubber gloves when I'm masking to keep the oil from my skin from touching the car.

An image that you would like mirrored on both sides, like scallops, is done by first drawing the pattern on two sheets of transfer paper and then laying the paper on the surface. Transfer paper has a thin, sticky coat on the back that acts like tape and paper combined. I like to draw the image about 1/16 larger than desired and then run a thin border of fine-line tape over the exposed edges of the transfer paper. This seems to provide a little cleaner look than just transfer paper by itself.

Graphics are usually done by freehand with an airbrush. This skill is even beyond most professionals' ability and requires years of experience to perfect. Most people will first base coat the primary color and then take the car to an airbrush artist for any graphics work.

RUNS AND OTHER PROBLEMS

Problems with temperature, flash time, viscosity and coat thickness are the primary reasons for runs. Few paints set up well below 70 degrees. The lower the temperature, the longer the flash time. Some paints won't cure at all below 50 degrees. In cold weather, you may need to double the amount of time you wait before applying another coat. Professional painters use heated spray booths to speed cure times and create a good painting environment all year round. When a coat of primer, sealer, paint, etc., is

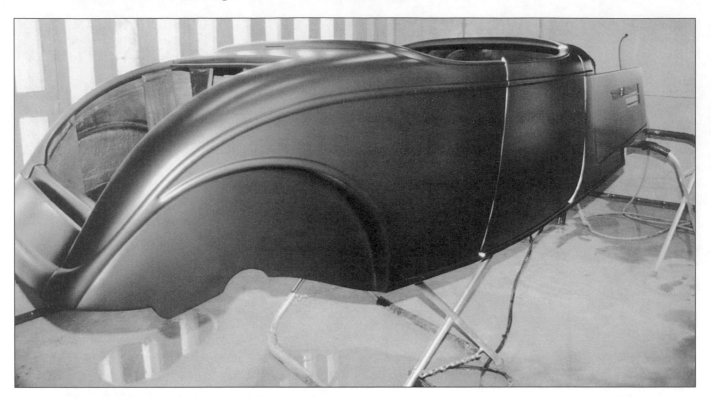

(courtesy of Gibbon Fiberglass Reproductions)

Base coat is applied over the sealer. It is highly reduced and runny so it is best to apply in thin, see-through coats to prevent runs. This technique helps the metallic flake lay down properly.

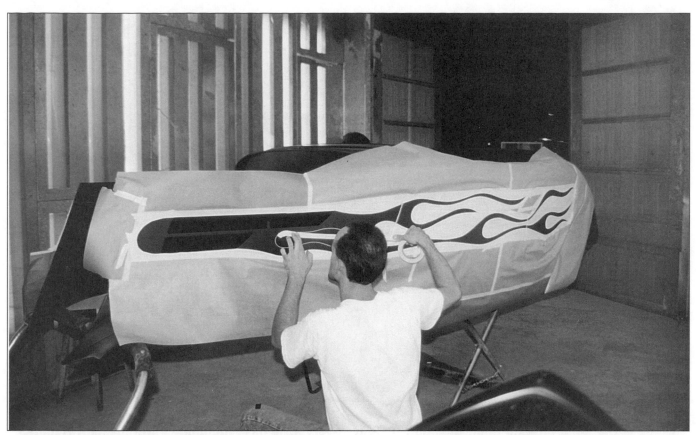

(courtesy of Gibbon Fiberglass Reproductions)

Scallops and flames should be taped off before the surface has been clear coated and after the base coat has fully dried. Base coat has a time window in which the clear coat must be applied. Here, Scott Manfull masks off an area for flames over this base coat.

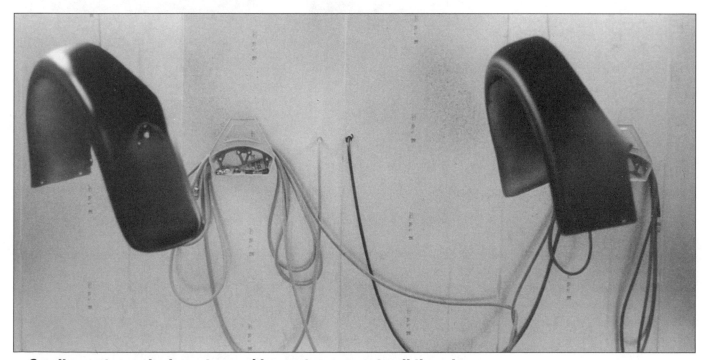

Smaller parts can be hung to provide greater access to all the edges.

(courtesy of TL Rod and Custom)

Black is the most difficult color to shoot. It shows every little flaw, including scratches, swirl marks and the slightest dent or flutter in the bodywork. Only the most experienced paint and body men work with dark colors. Pin striping has added to the detail and overall theme of this street rod.

(courtesy of TL Rod and Custom)

Pin striping is a great way to add detail to your paint, but it is not easy to apply. It requires a great deal of artisan skill to lay pin strip patterns by hand. Here, Gary Mizar hand lays a pattern on the trunk lid of this car.

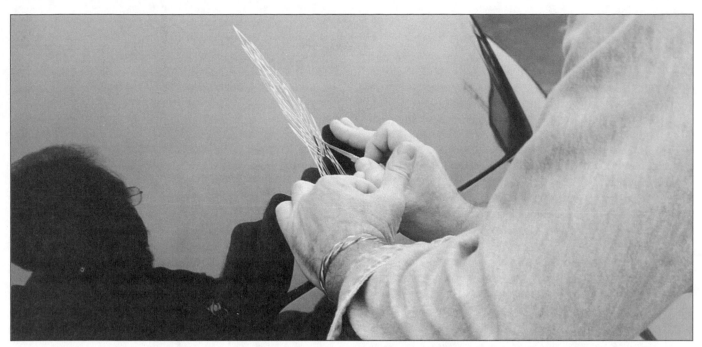

Hand laying complex patterns like this is extremely difficult to do. Gary also creates concept drawings to assist in theme planning and can be contacted through TL Rod and Custom.

applied, the surface will look wet. The time it takes for the reducer to flash off or evaporate, is called flash time. If you put two wet coats on top of each other, you'll get runs, so allow each coat to flash off properly. A normal flash time is about 10 minutes at 75 degrees, with this time increasing/decreasing with the ambient air temperature.

Some painters mix their paint too thin in an effort to reduce orange peel. This technique works, but at the risk of runs. This essentially turns the paint into the same viscosity as lacquer, so the VOC content becomes higher than what was designed by the manufacturer. The main drawback to doing this is that your flash time increases, thereby exposing the surface to contaminants longer. You will also need twice as many coats, and the paint will "shrink" over time.

Just about any product that has a reducer added can and will shrink as it cures. What happens is that the surface will be dry, but reducer is still slowly evaporating out of the paint. This can be a problem if you have over reduced all of your primer coats as well. It's frustrating when you finish your paint and go through the labor of color sanding and buffing the surface, only to have the surface look dull and pitted a month later. This happens when the products are over-reduced.

Fish eyes are caused when an oily contaminant is on the surface of the car before applying paint. When the paint hits this spot, it will push itself away from the contaminant and make a little circle that resembles a fish eye. This is a serious flaw and the entire surface will have to be wet sanded and resprayed. If this happens frequently, add an additional wax and grease remover step, use a different wax and grease remover, or try adding a small amount of fish eye eliminator liq-

uid to the paint itself. Your paint supplier can help you find one that is compatible to your paint brand.

If sanding scratches can be seen in the paint after it has been polished, then you are not working your primer/surfacer up into finer grits of sand paper as you block. You will need to add additional sanding steps to your process to cut the larger scratches down. It is easy to miss scratches if the surface does not have a guide coat to show you how much primer will need to be removed.

HOT PARTS

Parts that heat up need to be painted differently. Engine blocks and radiators should have one coat of epoxy primer and just enough paint to cover the primer. This is one place where the thinner the paint the better. Should an engine pan or radiator have a dent you would like to repair, first tap the dent from the back side the best you can and then use J B Weld instead of traditional body filler. Once dry, the J B Weld can be sanded flush and reprimed with epoxy. Whether or not you should use a base coat/clear coat system on these hot areas is debatable. I've seen several engine blocks shot in metallic paints with no problems. Some base coats don't withstand heat well, so ask your paint manufacturer if their base coats can be applied to engines. Neither of these paints will hold up on exhaust manifolds and are marginal on brake calipers. Special high-temperature paints can be purchased from Eastwood for the more extreme applications, like exhaust manifolds and systems.

As long as your bodywork has been done correctly, and you're clean and safe, you can be a good painter in time. This is one of those skills where practice makes perfect. Even the best painters make mistakes from time to time, so be patient if it doesn't come to you right away.

High-temperature areas require
different painting techniques.
High build primers are replaced
with one coat of epoxy and then
two or three coats of urethane paint.

(courtesy of Street Rods by Michael)

Radiators have plagued people for years.
I often see gorgeous engine compartments
with dented radiators. Radiators get too hot for
conventional body fillers, but there is a trick to
get around this. Have your local radiator shop
separate the top tank and give it to you. Using
normal hammer and dolly techniques, lightly
tap out the dents and have the shop solder
the tank back on. After the metal has been
cleaned, spread JB Weld over the dents
instead of body filler and sand normally.
A few heavy coats of epoxy primer can be
wet sanded for a smooth surface and painted.

Chapter 10

Color Sanding and Polishing Paint

Urethane paints are the industry standard and can be polished just as fine as the old lacquers, but any bumpy surfaces, or orange peel, must be removed first. This process is called "color sanding." Color sanding is just a fancy term for wet sanding the paint. There are many flaws or problems that can arise with paint, but three of them can be repaired in the color sanding process: runs, dust specs and orange peel.

All three flaws can be repaired, but runs are the most serious and difficult to fix. A run will form whenever more paint is applied to a surface than it can hold. Applying thick coats, poor spraying or coverage technique, cold temperature, improper gun setup and over-reduced paint can all cause runs. However, overcompensation can create dry or orange-peeled paint, so there is a balance that must be achieved. Some paints lay out flatter than others. Some are easy to run. Others are almost impossible to run but dry with severe orange peel. Every painter has a different preference.

REPAIRING RUNS

Some runs can be repaired before the color sanding process. Many painters will take a new razor blade and

scratch the run off once the paint has cured. This is done by laying the blade on top of the run, perpendicular to the surface, and lightly scratching back and forth in the direction of the run. The run will begin to look dull as the layers are scratched off. Great care must be given to avoid scratching the paint on either side of the run as the paint is not very thick there. One trick that will help is to take a small grinder and file the sharp corners off each end of the blade. This should help reduce damaging scratches. As you continue to lightly scrape away at the run, the dull, scratched area gets wider. This scratching process should be repeated until all of the run has been removed and the spot is flush with the surrounding area. Then continue with the normal color sanding process. This technique will not work 100 percent of the time and takes some practice, but it can save a lot of time once perfected.

COLOR SANDING

Color sanding removes the minor flaws of dust particles and orange peel in the paint. Urethane paints have a curing time that's based on heat, and they get harder as the curing process develops. Professional painters

The entire time you are color sanding and polishing, make sure the surface is free of all grit. Constantly wash the surface and check for grit with your hands.

Start wet sanding with 1000 grit to break the surface and finish removing orange peel with 1500. A light sanding with 2000 grit will make polishing easier.

Between every four or five strokes, dry the surface with a squeegee and check to see if the orange peel has been removed. Rinse the surface with water and repeat sanding if necessary.

Other tools are available like this paint nib file. These are used to cut down larger pieces of dirt in the paint before color sanding.

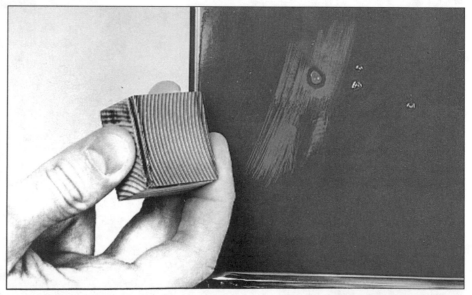

(courtesy of The Eastwood Company)

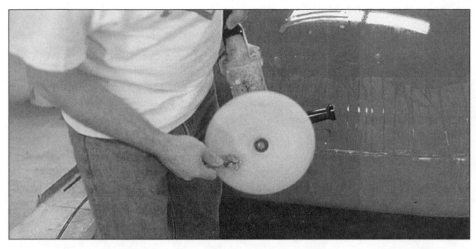

Buffing pads pick up dirt and dust from the air. Store them in a plastic bag or container when not in use. Wool pads should be cleaned with a spur before polishing and foam pads can be hand washed.

have spray booths that heat the paint to more than 150 degrees. At this temperature, urethane paint takes less than an hour to cure. If you lightly press your fingernail to the surfaces of the paint and it leaves a mark, then the paint has not cured enough for color sanding. However, if you wait too long, the paint will get so hard that the polishing process becomes difficult. You want to be polishing as soon as the paint has cured.

You must have a clean surface to color sand and polish paint. The smallest piece of grit can get trapped between the sandpaper and paint and cause damaging scratches. Wash the surface off before any work begins.

3M has a 6-inch wet sanding block that is perfect for color sanding. Using a block and 1,000-grit wet sand paper, lightly sand the surface of the paint. Sand only a few strokes and then dry the surface with a rubber squeegee. Look at the light reflection on the surface carefully. You should see just the tops of the orange peel sanded and turning dull and the low spots of the orange peel untouched and shiny looking. Color sanding is done in small sections at a time, approximately 6 by 6-inch areas at a time. Rinse water over the area and repeat

the process until the shiny low spots get noticeably smaller but do not disappear. You then switch to a 1,500-grit paper and continue to color sand until all of the low, shiny spots have disappeared. Lightly color sand the area again with 2,000 grit before any polishing begins. It is up to the builder whether they want to finish a small area through all the grits or finish an entire section, meaning body, hood, fenders, etc. with one grit at a time. Most painters will finish an entire section one grit at a time. Don't be alarmed if it seems you are using a lot of sandpaper. This is normal. Urethane is hard on sandpaper. You may go through 30 sheets or more.

Obviously, this process takes a lot of time, so many painters will opt to paint cars in sections. For example, paint and polish the body first and then move on to the fenders next. This way you always work with fresh paint, which is softer and easier to work with.

POLISHING

Polishing works in stages, much like color sanding. There are different grits of polishing compound to match the hardness of the paint. I use a fairly soft paint,

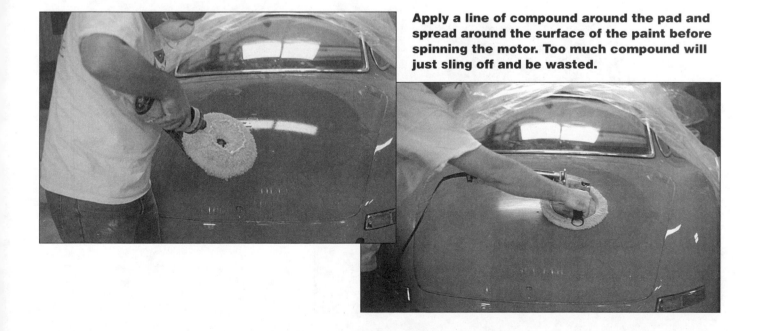

Apply a line of compound around the pad and spread around the surface of the paint before spinning the motor. Too much compound will just sling off and be wasted.

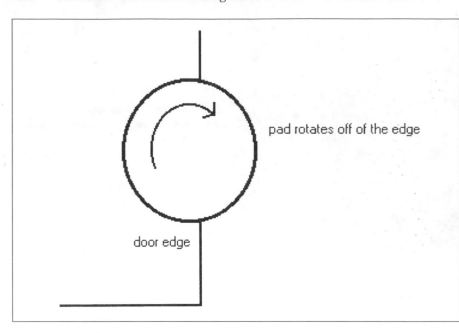

pad rotates off of the edge

door edge

The foam polishing technique is the same as using the wool pad. Be sure to watch the direction that the pad is traveling. Always polish off of an edge and cover sharp edges like drip rails with masking tape for protection.

There should be enough compound to polish 12" by 24" area back and forth. Make sure you do not stay in any one place too long, as you will overheat and burn the paint.

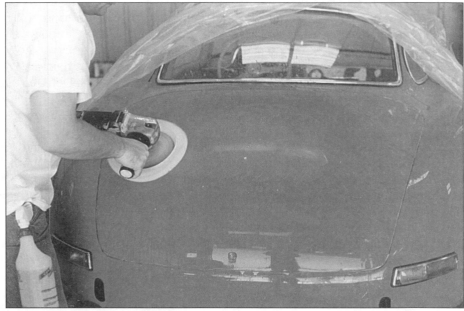

A mist of water can be used to cool and lubricate the surface if the compound begins to dry out.

Wool polishing pads leave fine swirl marks in the paint, Foam polishing pads and a special compound are used to remove these.

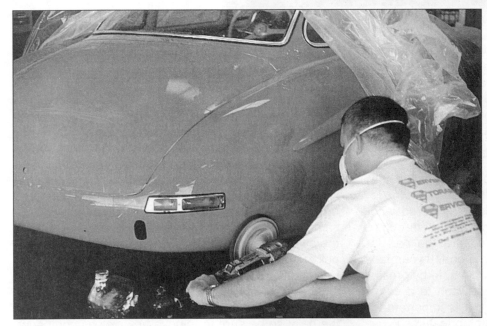

The foam polishing technique is the same as using the wool pad. Be sure to watch the direction that the pad is traveling. Always polish off of an edge and cover sharp edges like drip rails with masking tape for protection.

After polishing, study the surface reflection of a light source. By moving your head from left to right, you will be able to pick up slight imperfections such as sanding scratches or missed orange peel in the reflection. Show cars are void of any such imperfections. Expect to pay $1,500 to $3,500 for color sanding and polishing in most shops depending on the size of the vehicle and depth of detail you are looking for.

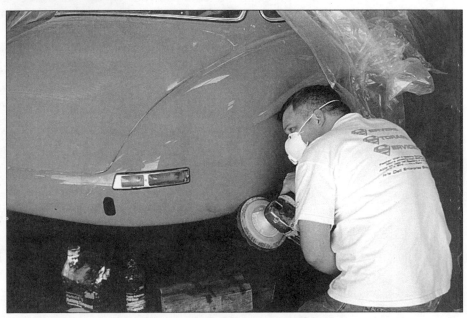

You can see the difference between the fender and the trunk lid. The trunk lid is not reflecting the ceiling lights like the top of the fender. You can read newspaper print in the reflection of a show car, but this may not be practical for most custom cars.

so I begin the polishing process with 3M Finesse-it II, which has no abrasive grit, and a wool buffing pad. Other paints may require some abrasive like 3M Imperial compound to start out with, so do not hesitate to call your paint supplier and get recommendations.

It is easy to "burn" an edge when you are buffing paint. This means that you buffed all the paint off and it can happen quickly if you are not careful. When you buff paint, always be conscious of the direction the pad is traveling. Sharp edges that the pad will come in contact with, like drip rails, should be covered with several layers of tape to prevent a burn-through. When you approach edges, make sure the pad is swirling off of the edge and never into one. If your pad is not polishing the paint, don't compensate by pressing down on the paint harder, just switch to a compound that has some abrasive in it. It is important to always keep the surface of the paint lubricated so you do not overheat and damage the paint. You can pre-

vent this by moving your pad around the entire section and buff in stages. Do not try to bring a small spot to a high luster in one pass. Keep plenty of compound on the surface and occasionally mist the surface with water to keep the area wet and cool.

On sunny days, you may have noticed that many dark-colored cars have swirl marks in the paint. These are very fine scratches that are usually caused by the owner during the cleaning and waxing process. The slightest dust particle trapped between the paint and rag can cause these. The wool polishing pads leave the same marks, so another process is needed to remove the swirl marks. 3M makes a foam polishing pad and polish just for this purpose. The surface needs to be free of other polishing compounds or dust, but the technique is the same used with wool pads. Some compounds have a chemical that can eventually damage the paint so be sure to remove any excess compound as soon as you are finished.

Chapter 11

Interiors

There is a lot of work on custom cars that owners can do themselves, but when we get to upholstery, there are limitations. Many models have interior kits available for as little as $500. These kits would provide an OEM-style interior that you could install yourself with a minimal tool investment. The door, trunk and kick panels either snap or screw into place. The carpet can be glued down using a 3M 8080 spray glue and the seat covers slip over the old padding and hog ring in place. Sure, the price is right, but these kits are all OEM, which kind of defeats the purpose in a custom car. To get custom work, you will have to take your car to an upholstery shop. There are custom interior specialists all over the country and prices start around $3,500 and can go over $10,000, depending on how elaborate you want to get. The average upholstery job costs around $5,000.

We'll use a shop in Alexander City, Alabama, to understand the interior process better. Shannon Walters, owner of Interiors by Shannon, has been working with custom upholstery for years and has several tips to simplify planning and reduce cost.

Upholstery begins with the wind lace and headliner installation. Most cars use some kind of cloth headliner to reduce cost, but any material could be used. Most of the seat fitting and consoles are manufactured before the carpet is installed. This is done mostly just to keep the carpet clean. There's no need to walk on the carpet and possibly damage it while the interior is in a construction phase.

Carpet is found in two primary materials: wool and nylon. Wool is frequently used in show cars, but the extra expense is not necessary for most custom cars.

MASTER CYLINDER

Some hot rods have master cylinders mounted under the floor so you have two options to add brake fluid — you can cut a hole in your carpet to give you a flip-up tab, or install a remote filler tube to give you access in the engine compartment. If you go with the

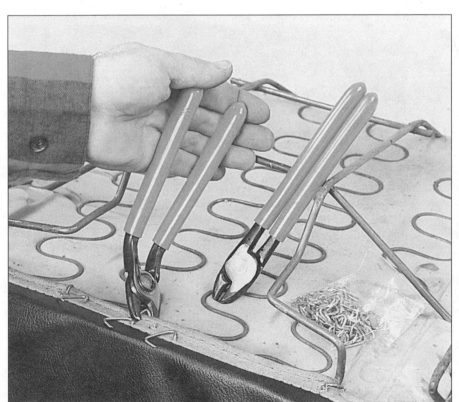

If you opt to re-cover your seats using a kit, you will need hog ring pliers and a bag of steel hog rings to clamp the fabric in place.

(courtesy of the Eastwood Company)

(courtesy of Interiors by Shannon)

A traditional bench seat was used to get a nostalgic look. Note the panel between the seat and the floor. Subtle details really set a car out from the rest.

first option, it is only a matter of time before you stain the carpet. Remote filler tubes and master cylinders add about $200 and can be worth every penny. Most models have a door sill plate that covers the edge of the carpet along the door openings. The upholsterer will need these to install the carpet and many styles can be purchased from Valley Auto Accessories and other companies.

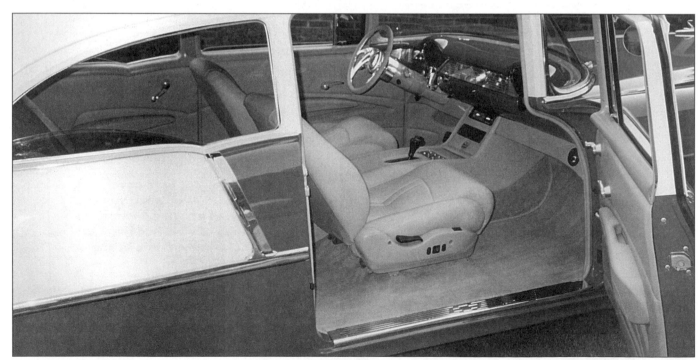

(courtesy of Interiors by Shannon)

Door sill plates can be purchased or custom made, but the upholsterer needs them ahead of time to finish the job.

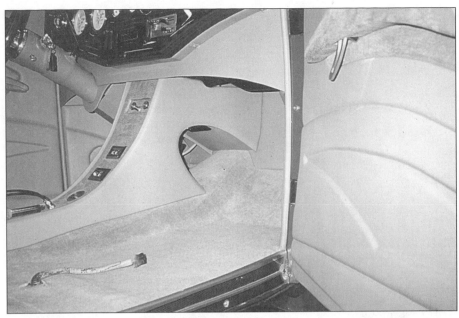

Consoles are both useful and attractive, but require planning when it comes to wiring. The cord coming out of the carpet is for power seats.

(courtesy of Interiors by Shannon)

DASH

When designing a custom dash, be aware that the dash cannot rest flush against the door. Many vehicles have a 1/2-inch-thick wind lacing around the door that lies between the A pillar and the dash. The door panels are 3/4 inch thick as well and could be more depending on how complicated you make them. Dashes can be painted or covered in material. OEM dashes were painted all the way through the 1950s and seem to still be very popular at the shows. SEM makes an aerosol paint for vinyl which works well on metal, too. It matches both the color and gloss of leather and is ideal for seat frames, garnish moldings and dashes.

WIRING TIPS

Interior design and electrical wiring work together much like the body and chassis do. One is dependent on the other. An interior design must be sketched out

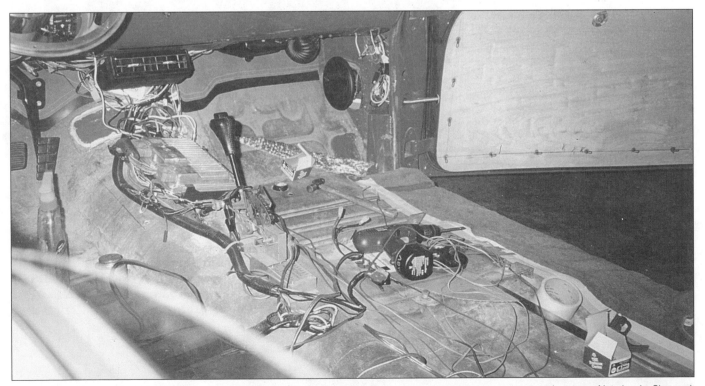

(courtesy of Interiors by Shannon)

The center area of the car is being wired for a console. This custom will have digital gauges, an aluminum steering wheel, air conditioning and speakers in the kick panels.

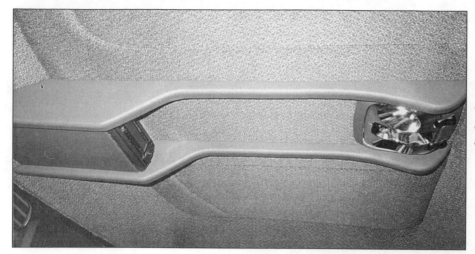

This tweed headliner has a console for overhead lights and stereo.

(courtesy of Interiors by Shannon)

When finished, the console holds the stereo, air conditioning, power windows and transmission shift lever.

(courtesy of Interiors by Shannon)

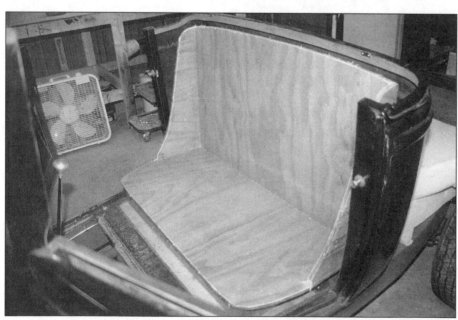

Sometimes consoles and seats have to be custom made out of plywood. They are molded with interior foam and covered like any other part.

(courtesy of Gibbon Fiberglass Reproductions)

(courtesy of Gibbon Fiberglass Reproductions)

Seats can either be re-mounted, or made from scratch, like this one.

before any wiring can take place. For example, will your car have power windows and if so, where will the switches be? Where will the speakers be mounted? Will you run your stereo up to a console in the ceiling, dash, floor or trunk? This all needs to be planned out. Then the vehicle wiring must be finished before the interior can begin.

Shannon Walters recommends that you leave slack in all of your wires just in case the upholstery shop needs to make adjustments. This is easily done by using plastic ties and running loops near the end of each wire. This will give 4 inches of play just in case, and be sure to leave slack in the entire wiring harness. There is no advantage to running your wires tight. If you are concerned about them moving around, then use plastic ties every foot or so to hold the wiring harness in place.

The small panel down by your feet between the door and the firewall is called the kick panel. There needs to be enough slack so the wires can travel from the dash up over these panels and out to the doors. Your heater hoses should have slack in them for the same reason. Many people like to run these under the dash, to the kick panels and out through the inner fender well area to avoid cutting any holes in the firewall. This is for aes-

thetic reasons only, but if you do this, install a metal spring in the hose where sharp bends occur to keep the hose from collapsing.

INSULATION

Be sure to put insulation in your car before taking it to the upholsterer. Insulation can be purchased from places like Yogi's Inc. and is easy to install. The insulation comes in stock sheets about 1/4-inch thick and can be cut to fit all of the flat surfaces inside the car. The door skins, firewall, floor, trunk, etc., are all prime candidates for this treatment. You will be surprised how much difference this insulation makes. Not only is road noise reduced, but vibration and little squeaks seem to disappear as well. The whole quality of the ride improves.

SEATS

There are a couple of factors to consider when installing seats. As far as planning goes, seatbacks without headrests should not rise higher than the bottom of the door window. In other words, if you are looking at the outside of the car, you should not see the seats above the window edge, and double check to see that the seatbacks are the same height. This is

(courtesy of Interiors by Shannon)

When going without headrests, it is a good idea to keep the seat backs flush with the top of the door. This gives an overall clean, sharp appearance.

for aesthetics more than functionality. The seats need to be mounted level and square to the car. Special care needs to be given to bucket seats to make sure the tracks are in the same place on either side of the car. When mounting old seats, make sure you com-

pensate for worn or missing cushion material. New foam will leave you about an inch higher than the exposed seat frame. This new foam will also be on the sides of the seat, so factor this in so the seats do not rub on the door panels. If you are using old seat

Factory door handles and window cranks are used to maintain a traditional look. It is important not to mix themes. Notice how traditional gauges help tie the theme together.

(courtesy of Interiors by Shannon)

(courtesy of Interiors by Shannon)

This design mixes tweed and vinyl. The wind lace around the door is clearly visible.

frames, save some money and remove all of the old material. There is no reason to pay somebody else to do that.

WINDOWS

All of the windows need to be installed, adjusted and working before the upholsterer can finish the job. Have you ever seen the brown bubbles that form on the edges of old automotive glass? There is a chemical in some window adhesives that attacks the plastic in laminated glass. Walters has a tip to prevent this: Put a thin coat of aquarium sealant around the edge of the glass before you put it in the frame. This will keep the window adhesive from touching the lamination. Aquarium sealants have silicon in them, so make sure you use them sparingly and away from any areas that painting is done. The window felting needs to be installed and the garnish moldings painted and fitted ahead of time.

UPHOLSTERY STYLES

Once you get to the upholsterer, there are some choices involved in the styling of the interior. The first choice involves the kind of material

(courtesy of Interiors by Shannon)

The interior theme has been carried to the trunk and trunk lid. This amount of detail is expected in show cars.

Notice how the door panel design travels down to the kick panel.

(courtesy of Interiors by Shannon)

you will use. Cloth or fabric is the least expensive of the materials and has the widest selection of patterns and colors. In custom cars, tweed is used frequently and is ideal for headliners, doors, etc. Tweed is a little harder to clean, so you may want to consider something smooth like vinyl or panel board on areas your feet touch, like kick panels. You do not see too much cloth in the trunk area mainly because the trunk is rarely seen, but show cars are expected to have this area finished to the same detail as the rest of the car and this usually means leather. Most people carry the interior theme to the trunk, but this is an easy place to cut back in order to meet budgets. Trunk mats and panel board are nice, affordable replacements.

Vinyl became popular in the 1950s as an inexpensive way to simulate leather. The old sales brochures are fun to read because vinyl was given all kinds of names that sound like animal hide, like leatherette, morokide or nagahyde. Vinyl has some practical uses, too. It resists water damage, which makes it ideal for convertibles and boats. However, the cost of leather has been coming down, so if you like the way it looks and feels, it adds about $1,000 to the total cost. This may be a critical planning issue because you see the interior every time you get in the car, but rarely crawl underneath. It makes sense to put the money where it will be most appreciated. Why spend $1,000 extra for an assortment of chrome or polished chassis parts under the car and then cut back on what is highly visible? The factory often

Even this rear package shelf has been done in leather.

(courtesy of Interiors by Shannon)

The French seam is visible on the front seat. The individual lines on the back seat are not top stitched. These are separate pieces of leather sewn together with plain seams.

(courtesy of Interiors by Shannon)

made subtle compromises to reduce cost. You frequently saw leather used on seats and vinyl placed on the dash, trunk, door panels, etc. Done correctly, the differences are very difficult to detect.

Decoration within the material itself is done several ways. Patterns can be sewn in the material with thread to visually break up large areas. Pleats are used the same way, but usually have to be used in straight lines. Buttons, beads and rhinestones have all been used, but are very uncommon in street rods. The factory would often mix colored fabrics and stitch them together. Most of the 1950s cars were done this way, where the border of the seat would be the primary color and an insert was stitched in to give contrast. This is still very popular on custom cars today and is done with all materials.

Different stitching can be used to add detail, too. Top stitching is the technique used to sew patterns or designs into the material. Different-colored thread can add to the effect because the thread is visible. The stitch is not used to join two pieces of material, it is only used for decoration. A plain stitch is used to join material, and the thread is not visible as it is under material. Plain stitching is used to create patterns similar to top stitching, but is much more time consuming for the upholsterer. Instead of using one piece, the upholsterer must measure and cut smaller pieces and join them together so they appear to be one piece. This is very popular in custom cars. Welt cord was used in the seams at the factory, but seems to fallen out of favor in the customizing world. You may want to use it if you are

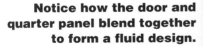

Notice how the door and quarter panel blend together to form a fluid design.

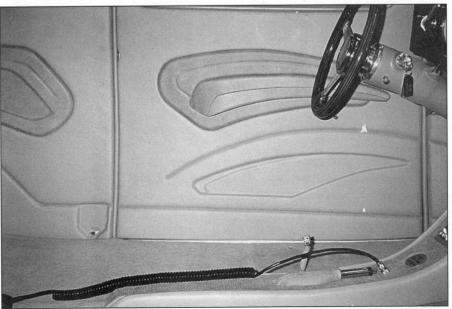

(courtesy of Interiors by Shannon)

(courtesy of Interiors by Shannon)

Notice how both door panels are symmetrical. The lines in the panel are created by separate pieces of leather plain stitched together. You cannot see the thread this way.

seeking a nostalgic look. French seams are very popular and have stitched thread on either side of the seam, much like a baseball. Small logos and personalized designs are done with embroidery. It's common to see car logos like the Chevy bowtie stitched into the seats as an accent.

You pay for detail in upholstery much the way you do with paint. So remember, the more elaborate your

design, the more it will cost. Like paint, it is a good idea to get a reference or see the quality of the shop's work before you begin. An interior package takes four to six weeks to complete, and that may be a factor if you are rushing to get to a show. Always check the shop's availability several months in advance and ask to be put on their schedule. The better shops will have months of work lined up at any given time.

Chapter 12

Restoring Trim

The decision on whether to restore trim and the planning of an overall theme go hand in hand. The trim includes bumpers, lenses, OEM emblems, stainless moldings, hood ornaments, etc. Try to design a theme that is consistent. Are you building a modern "high-tech" look or going with a nostalgic one? Putting in digital gauges, removing the bumpers and keeping the OEM stainless moldings will appear out of balance. Designing the trim layout up front is critical to the overall success of the project.

Chrome continues to get more expensive every year. I've worked on cars that had $20,000 in chrome work alone. Any car from the '50s will be covered in an assortment of chrome and stainless. All of these orna-ment and molding locations have holes drilled into the steel. The holes will need to be welded up if you intend to delete the trim, so if you wait until after the car is painted to make a decision it's too late.

Many hot rodders choose to eliminate all the OEM trim and create their own. All kinds of creative parts can be cut out of stainless stock and polished to look OEM. Most winning show cars incorporate custom-made trim. It's the only way to really ensure that you have a "one-of-a-kind" appearance.

If you are trying to keep a budget under control or reduce expenses, then go with a clean, stripped-down look. Many custom car builders use the monochro-matic look successfully. You may choose to remove all

(courtesy of Kemps Rod & Restoration)

Both the grill and hood inserts have been custom manufactured out of stainless steel. This is almost expected in the higher-caliber show cars.

(courtesy of Interiors by Shannon)

This rod is using an original style chrome bumper, but incorporated the body color in the insert.

(courtesy of Gibbon Fiberglass Reproductions)

Here is an example of a custom-built bumper. It won't protect much, but it looks sharp.

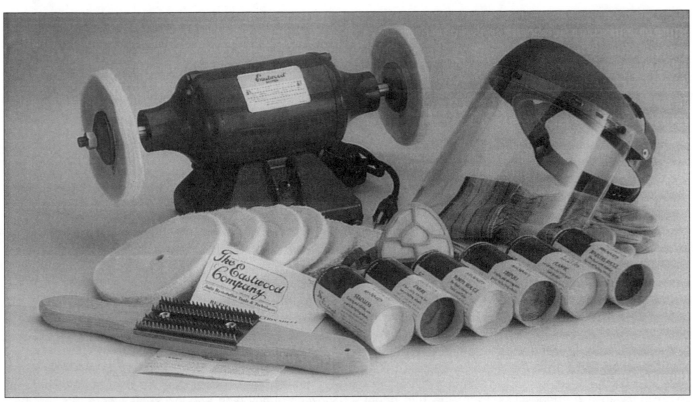

(courtesy of the Eastwood Company)

Complete buffing kits like this one can be purchased for about $500. They polish all kinds of metals and plastics.

Aluminum is soft and easy to polish. You can polish headers, valve covers and manifolds yourself.

(courtesy of the Eastwood Company)

(courtesy of the Eastwood Company)

Most buffing kits come with plastic compound and a small wheel. As long as the plastic isn't cracked, it can be restored.

of the trim and weld up the holes or paint all of the trim body color. You could have a metallic emerald green body and paint the trim a darker shade of green and come out with a gorgeous car. Paint the trim bright yellow and you may have a different story, but there is a lot of room for artistic expression.

If you stay with chrome, it will have to be sent to a professional, but you can save money by doing other trim restoration yourself. For example, aluminum parts can be bought polished or unpolished. Valve covers, headers, intake manifolds, etc., could all be polished by the builder himself. Buffing kits complete with motor, wheels and compounds can be purchased around

$500. The theory behind polishing metal is the same as polishing paint: You work your part in stages using different wheels and compounds until the desired luster is achieved. Different metals require different compounds depending on how hard the metal is. Your kit comes with instructions explaining which compound and technique to use for a given metal.

The trim running down the side of the vehicle is perhaps the most difficult to restore because it is thin and usually dented. Up until the 1960s, this trim was almost always made out of stainless steel. Stainless is about as hard a metal as you can find on a car, but it can be restored. If the metal has large dents or has been crushed, it is probably beyond repair, so check to see if the part is being reproduced. If not, you will need to find a replacement from a salvage yard. However, scratches, chips and dime-size dents can all be repaired.

Dents need to be addressed first. A small body hammer and anvil are used to tap the dent from the inside out. This tapping process should be done a little at a time until the dent becomes flush with the anvil. When you feel the dent has been worked out, inspect the trim by running your fingers over the dent. You should feel dozens of tiny high and low spots where the dent has been worked out. If the whole area feels high or raised up, that is an indication that you have been tapping too hard or haven't kept the trim flush against the anvil. You can check your work by sanding the outside of the steel with a dual-action sander and 320-grit paper. The high spots will scratch first, leaving the low spots untouched. The differences between the two should be very slight and you may need to work some areas again. Then sand the area so that all high and low spots have been

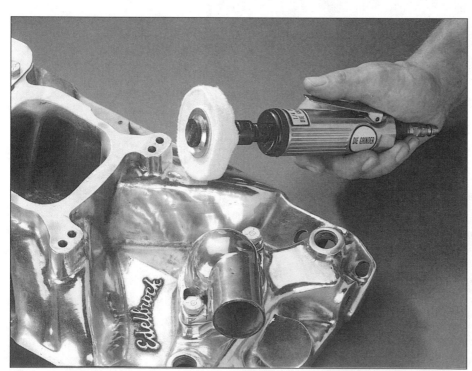

Die grinders are excellent all-purpose tools. With different attachments they can be used to polish, cut and grind.

(courtesy of the Eastwood Company)

removed. You literally cut the surface down so the whole area is flush with the lowest point. This should tell you that the difference between the high and low spots can be no greater than the thickness of the steel itself or you will end up with holes in the metal. The technique takes practice but ultimately isn't difficult to perfect. The 320-grit paper will remove the scratches and small nicks too.

The 320-grit scratches then have to be removed. Most dual-action sanders have a locking mechanism that converts them to grinders. Use 400-grit paper and a grinder to lightly work over all of the 320 scratches. The 400 grit is aggressive and will get the steel so hot that it can turn blue so constantly move the grinder around the surface to disperse the heat. Stop as soon as the circular scratches are gone. Repeat the process with 600- and 800-grit paper. The 800 grit is so smooth that the surface will almost look polished. You can inspect the surface once again to see if you're satisfied with the finish. Sometimes you will see wavy or distorted areas near the dent and these can be worked out again, but try to decide how far you want to go. It takes countless hours of tapping to get stainless "perfect." When you are satisfied that the scratches and dents are removed, you can finish polishing the steel with the stainless compounds provided in the buffing kit.

(courtesy of the Eastwood Company)

Polishers work best around waist height. A pedestal can be purchased for about $150 to make polishing large parts easier.

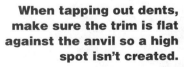

When tapping out dents, make sure the trim is flat against the anvil so a high spot isn't created.

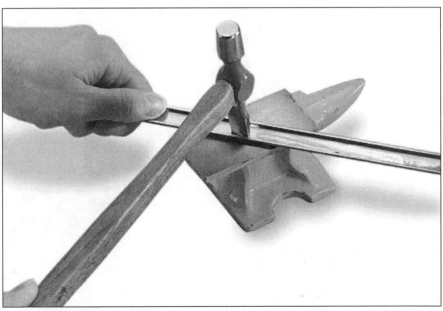

(courtesy of the Eastwood Company)

Chapter 13

Wrapping Up

There is a saying by people who build cars that the last 20 percent of the car takes 80 percent of the time to complete. We call this the 20/80 rule. This is an exaggeration, but it feels like it sometimes. Part of the problem is that you get excited after the car is painted and time seems to go by slower, but having a steady stream of parts finished and ready during the final assembly phase of the project can be challenging at times.

It's a good idea to get a jump on a couple of things before you get too close to the finish. Chrome plating can take several months, so send the chrome out around the same time you are doing bodywork. Around this same time, you should also order your wiring harness.

WIRING AND ACCESSORIES

Wiring a car intimidates a lot of people because they think you have to go down to Radio Shack, buy a spool of wire and build the harness from scratch. It can be done this way, but the sound of it intimidates me, too. There is

a much easier way. A complete wiring kit can be purchased from Affordable Street Rods for less than $300.

The basic idea for automotive wiring is the power comes off the battery through an ignition switch to the starter and power panel. The power panel (fuse panel) distributes the power to each individual circuit with a fuse for safety reasons.

Now, I've seen some rodders bypass the fuses to save time. Let's just say I unsuccessfully tried this very thing when I was in high school. Some months afterwards a short in the radio triggered a domino affect that rapidly set all of my wires in the car on fire. This normally would be enough to ruin your day, except this event happened at the exact same time I was being pulled over for a minor traffic violation. Well, the fire department showed up, next followed by my parents. It wasn't exactly my finest hour, but at least I learned some of my lessons early! Trust me, the fuses are there for a reason.

The nice thing about a kit is that the fuse box and wires are labeled so all you have to do is run the wires

Some power panels come with turn flashers built in and labeled for easy installation.

(courtesy of Affordable Street Rods)

to a location and hook them up to the appropriate number on the fuse box. It's pretty easy. When you order your kit, Affordable Street Rods will need to know what type of engine you have, whether it is fuel injected and how many power-operated accessories, such as power seats or windows, that you have.

There will be all kinds of odds and ends parts to order, like gauges, accessories and weather stripping. The Internet is obviously a good place to network from. Sites like www.hotrodhotline.com and www.hotrodsuperstore are great places to start. There is also a huge listing of suppliers at the back of this book. Most companies don't mind if you call them and ask for help. If you get stuck trying to find a part, pick up the phone and start calling companies. Chances are if they don't have it, they can recommend somebody to call. The key is to develop a project plan that delivers parts when you need them.

GLASS

Most hot rods have flat glass all the way around the car. This greatly simplifies glass installation. Most flat glass can be purchased and cut locally. As you move into the late 1940s and 1950s, auto manufacturers introduced curved glass and this presents a problem if your top is chopped. A good source for automotive glass is City Glass & Upholstery in Tacoma, Washington. In a pinch, I've cut curved glass myself using a diamond-coated cutoff disc and a Dremmel tool. As long as you cut very slowly and keep a stream of water running over the glass, you should be successful. Nothing with glass is 100 percent so make sure replacement glass can be purchased if you decide to do it yourself and make a mistake. Like steel, you can always cut more off if you need to, so be conservative with your measurements.

BE EXTRA CAREFUL

When installing components on your vehicle, protect painted surfaces with foam padding or masking tape. Installing hoods and trunk lids are perhaps the most difficult. Some makes are pretty heavy and it is easy to scratch fenders and body areas during installation. A layer of padding can save countless hours of work.

Painted or chrome-plated bolts can be protected by wrapping two layers of masking tape around the head

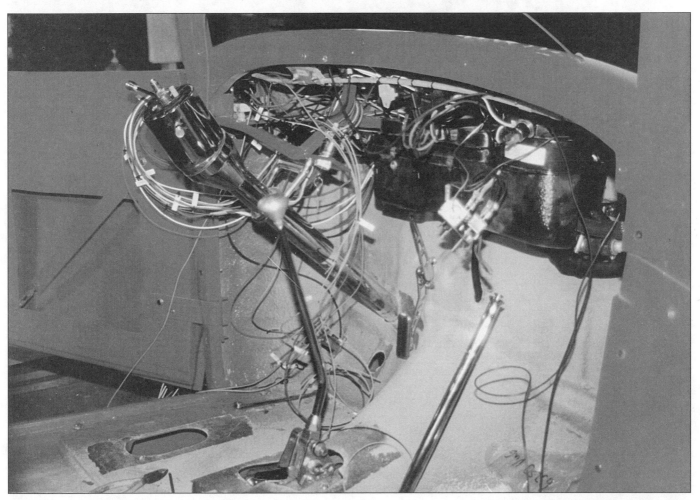

(courtesy of Gibbon Fiberglass Reproductions)

If your car has a removable dash, you will find it much easier working on the heater hoses, duct work and wiring on the firewall with the dash removed.

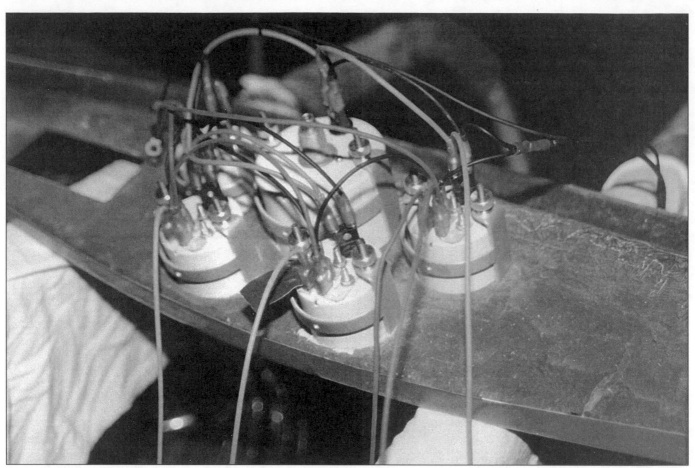

(courtesy of Gibbon Fiberglass Reproductions)

Instrument gauge clusters usually come with their own wiring harnesses to simplify installation. Most clusters come with the gas tank sending unit as well.

Masking tape can be used in several places to reduce the risk of damaged paint. Here, masking tape is placed around the hole for the radio antenna. The tape will help protect the surface until the antenna assembly has been test fitted. Tape can also be used around the heads of painted or chrome-plated bolts during assembly.

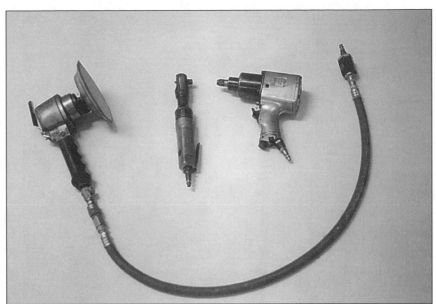

Power tools more than pay for themselves with the time they save. When it comes to the assembly phase, however, you are better off slowing down. Hand tools provide better control and reduce the risk of damaging painted surfaces.

before tightening. When using a wrench or ratchet near painted surfaces, hold the wrench with both hands and use one hand to cover the end of the tool. This technique will help keep the end of the tool from striking a painted surface during assembly.

As is the case when assembling fiberglass, do not over-tighten components that bolt to a painted surface. Nylon lock nuts should also be used to fasten stainless moldings, emblems, chrome, etc. If the part begins to make an impression into the paint, then you are tightening too hard.

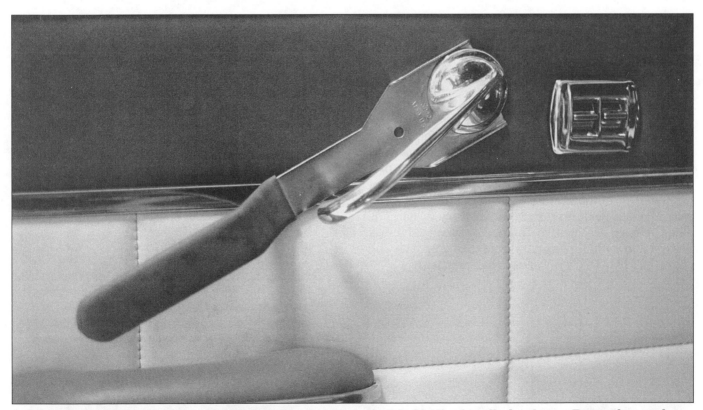

Most door handles have a retention spring or screw that holds the handle in place. Retention springs require a special tool to install and remove them.

Body panels frequently need shimming to line up properly. Shims can be made out of sheet metal or washers.

HAVE THE RIGHT TOOLS

Knowing when to use the right tool is key. Certain parts can only be removed or installed with specialized tools. Steering wheels, bearings, bezels and moldings are perfect examples. Never try to force a part on or off a car and risk damaging it. It may just need a different tool. Power tools are great time savers during the disassembly phase of a car, but once everything has been painted it is a good idea to slow down. Hand tools provide much more control and reduce the risk of damaging paint. Perhaps more mistakes are made by professionals trying to rush a car for a show than any other reason. Try not to force the situation. A car doesn't know what a calendar is so take your time and do things right. There will always be another show.

(courtesy of the Eastwood Company)

If you are having trouble removing your steering wheel, you may need a steering wheel remover. This tool pops them right off.

Chapter 14

Care and Maintenance

Once the car is finished, you'll probably ask yourself the question, "What do I do next?" Finishing a car takes countless hours and great perseverance. Many people immediately start new projects, because for them the fun is in the build process. I must admit that I fall into that group, but there is some final advice I would like to leave you with.

USE YOUR CAMERA

Take lots of photos throughout the project! As time goes by, I love to go through my old scrapbooks and see all the work that went into the cars. If you take your car to shows, leave the scrapbooks out for all to see. You will be surprised how much conversation will start. Who knows, if you document the project well enough, maybe you will be writing the next hot rod book. The photos will also be valuable if you ever want to sell the car. They should document all of the hard work as well as the quality that went into your vehicle.

SECURITY

On a darker note, your scrapbook will be invaluable should the car ever get stolen. Yes, you need to consider this. Street rods are prime candidates for theft. I can't tell you how many shows I've been to where cars get stolen right off the show grounds. Everytime it happens, we stand around and scratch our heads and ask why. The answer is easy — custom cars are easy to retool and sell. Usually a team of thieves will go to a show and steal multiple cars and bring them back to their shop. With the replacement of a few tags and a new coat of paint, they can register the car as a new build. Let's say your '37 Ford is stolen, all they need to do is purchase a rusty '37 and transfer those numbers to your car. Then wait six months so it looks like they worked on it and sell it for $20,000. Do this a dozen times a year and you are making a pretty good living with little work.

Car alarms are not good enough. I highly recommend that you consider something more advanced, like the Lo Jack system. This technology can be purchased for around $800. With this system your car gets registered in a national database. As soon as your car is reported missing, a signal is transmitted from the police radio network and activates a transmitter in your car. The police follow the signal and locate and retrieve the car for you. The system works so well that many thieves take stolen cars to vacant lots and let them sit. They watch from a distance and wait to see if police come to retrieve the car. They do this because they don't want to lure police to their shop, but the good news is you have a decent chance of getting your car back without a damaging high-speed chase.

Most of the time, you can clean your car by just dusting it off. After a few uses, just drop them in the washing machine and reuse them.

(courtesy of the Eastwood Co.)

A little common sense and extra care can keep your prize street rod safe and in A-1 condition.

STORAGE

Cars need to be driven, so another damaging factor is time and storage. A lot of cars sit throughout the winter and this is hard on a car. Winterize your vehicle by putting the car up on jack stands. This keeps the tires from cracking or developing flat spots. Most importantly, start your car once a week. Modern gasoline has a chemical in it that causes it to gel over time. There are chemicals you can add to your tank to prevent this, but nothing is healthier for an engine than for it to run. This keeps all of your gaskets wet and the moving parts lubricated. Avoid condensation in the tank by keeping it full. The less air in the tank the better. Armor All or silicon spray all the rubber gaskets to keep them form sticking to the steel or cracking.

WASHING

Most paint damage is caused by the owners. We have been taught all our lives to "wax-on/ wax-off" in circles, but this leaves that spider-web effect you see in dark-colored paint. The darker the color, the more noticeable they become. In fact, wax is not what you want to use on urethane paint, anyway. All enamels are softer than lacquer. Whenever you use wax, water beads up on the surface of the paint. These little beads act like magnifying glasses, and the sun will hit these beads and burn tiny marks in the surface of the paint. You are better off not to wash your car at all. If your car has been driven on wet roads or has mud caked on, then yes, you will have to wash it. But if a car is simply dusty, you can use a dust mop to pick up any loose dust particles and then use a hand glaze to bring out the luster in the paint. As long as you rub the glaze in straight lines down the length of the car, you will not get those circular spider web scratches in the paint. Dri Wash 'n Guard is another product that is catching on with rodders and it is used in lieu of hand glaze.

Most of all, rodding is about fun. Almost immediately after your car is finished, the first *Jackassus Maximus* will come out of the woodwork and probably tell you all the things that are wrong with your car. The problem with this subclass of the human species is they think know everything about hot rods, but don't seem to own one. The fact is, these bitter people are just jealous that you persevered and they didn't. You will meet a few of these, but most people in rodding love to have fun, so congratulations and enjoy!

Chapter 15

How to Inspect a Shop

A friend of mine asked me to tag along one day to visit a shop he was thinking of taking his car. I kept quiet and just wandered along with him as the owner showed us around the facility. It was impressive in the sense that it was large with 20,000 square feet or more and had at least two dozen cars in all stages of construction. All the cars were organized neatly in bays and there must have been eight employees all working diligently on various tasks. The shop was clean too, which is a real pet peeve of mine.

I know my friend was impressed and was excited to get on the waiting list to have the shop begin work on his car. On the way home, he asked me what I thought and I had to say that I would pass on doing business with this shop. He was surprised, but professionals have different criteria for judging shops than most customers.

I thought it might be useful to pass along some tips professionals use to evaluate other shops.

It is very rare to find a shop that performs every task of a project. First, the investment needed to do mechanical, electrical, upholstery, engine, transmission, paint, bodywork, etc. is cost prohibitive, and the chances that you could find stable employees that have mastered each or all of the skills are very slim.

Most shops focus on their individual specialization and farm certain "extras" out to other shops. For example, a good paint booth will cost between $30,000 and $100,000. Shops specializing in paint and bodywork usually farm out chrome, engine build and upholstery to other shops to save time and money. However, the shop that gets the car first is technically responsible for all the work the other shops do, so most professionals have certain things they look for when evaluating other shops.

There were things I liked about that shop. First, cleanliness is crucial. Dirty shops have a tendency to lose things. It's also a pride thing. If you don't have any pride in your shop, why should I expect you to take pride in your work?

I also like to see plenty of shelves near all the cars with bagged and labeled parts neatly stacked in place. There are some cars where certain replacement screws can cost hundreds of dollars, so you just can't afford to loose parts. You also have to consider that as time goes by, you won't remember what all the parts look like or where they go. Clearly labeled and neatly stored parts make the entire construction go smoothly. The same goes for the office. People that have paper piles all over the place also have a tendency to lose things.

Tim Lovvorn block sands a body panel. This shop is clean and appears to have plenty of room for the workers – two key considerations when selecting a shop.

(courtesy of TL Rod and Custom)

(courtesy of TL Rod and Custom)

When you tour a shop, do employees seem to be concentrating on thier work? Here Gary Mizar obviously is concentrating on, and cares about, his work.

Space is also important. When a car is completely disassembled, it can easily take up four times as much space. Shoebox-sized shops just don't seem to work well. About 600 to 800 square feet per car is needed to be effective. Pay special attention to the employees and how they are working. Hot rod building takes per-

severance and diligence. I have found that the two have a tendency to be polar opposites.

Perseverance has a tendency to come easy for employees. As long as they are getting paid, they can persevere through just about anything. It is different for hobbyists, however. It's hard to find free time to work on

This shop obviously has plenty of room and is neat and well organized. These are good indicators the shop has its act together.

(courtesy of Gibbon Fiberglass Repoductions)

Even with several projects going on at once and lots of parts and equipment around, a shop can be clean and professional-looking.

cars, especially if small children are anywhere in the picture. If a project stalls or gets set aside, it just seems too easy to abandon the project altogether. Diligence is something completely different. People seem to care more about things they own, but have a tendency to slack off a bit if it belongs to someone else. Employees may cut corners when the boss isn't looking and that is hard to control for shop owners. I know I fought it constantly! I study the employee to see if they are focused on their work or are they looking away or daydreaming. Do they seem to talk amongst themselves constantly or wander around the shop? I can't tell you how many times I've walked into a shop and have seen everybody drinking beer! There is work time and play time. Do they really mix? Would you want someone assembling your steering linkage after a six-pack? Any one of these things would be a deal breaker for me.

There are other things I look for too, like employee-to-car ratio. In this case, there were eight employees and 24 cars. If a complete project takes 1 or 2 years to complete when working full-time, then it's likely your car will sit in the shop 6 years or so if they have a 3:1 car to employee ratio. The only way to reduce that number is to cut corners and all too often that is what shops decide to do. I look for shops with a 1.5 car-to-employee ratio or less, so in our example, it

would be better if the shop had 8 employees and only 12 cars.

That was the first thing I noticed that I didn't like. The second was that I noticed that the shop had a racing team and I could see the trailer and racecar parked out back. Now, there are plenty of shops with race teams that produce good work, but I have had several negative adventures with them. In my experiences, it just seemed that the owners used the shop as a means to support their true passion, which was racing. I feel uncomfortable doing business with anyone who doesn't have all of their attention and resources focused on the work at hand. The attitude I got at several of these shops was "Yea, yea, just put it over there and we'll call you later with the estimate." That's not good enough for me and it seemed all of these shops were either overpriced or took too long to complete the work. I no longer do business with anybody that has a shop-supported distraction like racing.

The last tip is perhaps the most obvious, but seems to be overlooked because it takes time. Get a reference or referral. Let someone else be the guinea pig. It is crucial to speak with someone that actually did business with the shop before you and puts their personal recommendation on it. If there is a consistent problem with quality, billing or customer service, then the person before you probably knows about it.

Chapter 16

First-Time Success Story

To gain a better appreciation for what an "everyman" can expect when tackling their first custom car project, it might be a good idea to use one custom builder's first-time experience as a case study.

Paul Katzke is a retired resident of Iola, Wisconsin, and a lifetime car buff. He has owned and worked on many cars over the years. Before tackling his first custom project — a street rod truck for his wife — Katzke had built and restored several stock automobiles, including a 1947 DeSoto and 1966 Buick Skylark convertible.

Although Katzke's experience and expertise as a mechanic and car builder may surpass that of many rookie street rodders, he faced many of the same dilemmas and decisions that arise for any first-timer. In the end, Katzke followed a sound game plan: He did as much work himself as he could, went to professionals for the work he couldn't do himself (frame, paint, upholstery), and took his time.

After 7 years of work, he was able to present his wife with "The Cotton Candy Express," a sparkling, custom 1946 Chevy pickup that has evolved into an award-winning show vehicle.

Here's how he did it.

After 7 years of hard work, a rusting shell is turned into a trophy-winning 1946 gem.

A future treasure, complete with bird's nests where the headlights should be.

YOUR "TYPICAL" HOT RODDER

"I guess there are two types of hot rodders," Katzke said. "There are the investors, which I look down on. They pick up a car and rod it for a while, pick up a few trophies, and try to make some money.

"Then there is the guy who maybe has a wife and kids and is mechanically inclined. His fingers are always a little dirty. He can't really afford it, but … That's the way I was when I started. I was married and had four kids. I started out with a 1947 DeSoto that I bought for $25 because the people just wanted it the hell out of their garage!"

A DO-IT-YOURSELFER

Katzke estimates he did 95 percent of the work himself for his first hot rod project. He went to professionals for the paint and upholstery, the frame welding, and a few other specialty projects, such as a custom radiator.

The body is in decent shape, but the top of the cab will be replaced and the fenders and running boards will eventually be fiberglass.

Not much is salvageable on the front end.

After spending seven years building a truck for his wife, Katzke elected to have a professional shop do the work when it came to time to get his own high-performance street rod truck. "That's much more expensive," he said. "That came later for me. It's definitely cheaper to do it yourself. Definitely."

SELECTING A VEHICLE

Katzke had owned and worked on many vehicles over the years, including several old cars. But he hadn't taken on a big truck project until he turned to hot rodding.

"My wife, Bonnie, always wanted an old truck, and my son and I were always out at salvage yards looking for cars and car parts," Katzke recalled. "One day we ran across an old 1946 (Chevrolet) pickup truck, and I took her out and showed her and asked her if she wanted me to build the truck up for her.

"She said yes, and the deal was that I'll build it the way I want to build it and she could pick out the colors and the upholstery."

Katzke said it was also easier to find a truck than a car.

"She had always wanted an old truck, and I thought, 'Gosh, trucks are coming on strong. They're not all used up. And trucks are definitely easier to work on.' "

Katzke paid $125 for the truck "with the condition that I bring the engine back."

PARTS CARS

Katzke used a pair of unlikely donor vehicles for many of the parts for his '46 Chevy truck – a well-worn 1979 Chevy van that been the family vehicle for many years, and a 1973 Pontiac Ventura that he found in a local junkyard.

The van wound up providing the engine, transmission and various other goodies, while the Ventura provided the frame and suspension, among other things.

GETTING STARTED

Katzke hauled the vehicle home behind a homemade wrecker and dragged it into a barn on the farm he was renting. The truck was pretty solid in the body and frame, but the engine hadn't been run for years and was of no real use.

"We got it back to the barn and disassembled it – that's the fun part, disassembling it, but after that is when most people quit," Katzke said.

"The body was solid. The frame was solid, but the front end was junk. We gave the engine back … The cab was solid but the top was dented. We ended up getting another cab for $75 and putting that on."

SUBFRAME

The '73 Ventura provided the subframe, which Katzke cut out himself for $40. A professional welder

The cab and box are almost ready for paint, but plenty of works remains on the engine, front end and interior.

The engine is painted and chromed, but the firewall still needs some work.

The custom, stainless-steel firewall was taken from a semi truck. The modified radiator shell is also ready.

The dash remains from the '46 truck, complete with windshield crank.

attached it to the frame of the '46 truck. "I know how to weld, but I don't want to put my wife's life in my hands," Katzke said. "I let a professional handle the frame welding.

"In reality we had a '73 Ventura suspension holding up a '46 Chevy truck, which gave us power steering, power brakes, modern suspension and modern steering up front."

ENGINE

One of Katzke's most successful moves was his decision to breathe new life into his van engine. The 180-hp stock 350 soon became a bored-out hot rod engine rated at 305 hp. It features a 3/4-in. racing cam and lots of chrome.

"The van was getting old at the time, and it got to the point where we couldn't do anything with it anymore, so we pulled the 350 out and made it into a street and strip engine," Katzke said. "We used dish pistons to bring the compression down so we could use regular gas.

Beginning to wire the instrument panel and steering.

The new front end is beginning to take shape.

"The 350 is one of the most popular engines in the street rodding industry. Parts are readily available and it's such a versatile engine. There are so many manufacturers making aftermarket parts that there is kind of a price war going on."

The configuration of the front end required that the radiator shell be cut and narrowed by about 6 inches. A four-core radiator was then built from scratch by a specialist.

An electric fuel pump was installed with an emergency shut-off valve that cuts the fuel supply off when the oil pressure drops. "That's a safety feature," Katzke said. "You don't want to get into an accident and have the electric fuel pump still pumping gas. That can be bad."

TRANSMISSION

General Motors 350 TH transplanted from the Chevy van.

STEERING

The '46 truck's steering setup bears little resemblance to the original.

Another practice build. The engine and front end are nearing completion.

"As it happened, the '79 van has got a beautiful tilt steering wheel, and we took that out and bolted it right into the Ventura steering gear with no modifications. That was a little lucky, but a lot of planning also."

The truck operates with standard 1973 vintage variable-ratio power steering.

FUEL TANK

Katzke had to rig up his own fuel tank, primarily because he didn't want it located in the cab area, where it was originally.

"That's too dangerous," he said. "We built a tank and put it underneath the box. Then we took the sending unit and adapted it to the '46. It worked out beautifully."

The tank utilizes an electronically operated pop-up door located in the bed.

"We had to get fancy," Katzke said. "We didn't want it to be like a regular truck. We went to a salvage yard and got one of those little yellow buttons, like you find in glove compartments … and we made a door popper. The door is in the bed and that's where you fill the gas tank. That was my own idea."

WIRING AND FUSE BOX

"We had all the steering wheel wiring from the (van) and we went back and pulled out all the rest of the wiring harness and put it in the truck," Katzke said. "We saved a whole bunch of money doing that."

Katzke said he wasn't even tempted to buy new wiring harness.

"I knew we could make it work," he said. "I had built this thing in my mind over the last 20 years."

The fuse box remained under the dash where it had been originally.

FRONT END

"We basically pulled out the whole front end and started over," Katzke said. "New springs, joints … For all practical purposes it's an all-new vehicle up front."

HOOD

Katzke picked up the hood from a second donor 1947 Chevy truck, but took off the side curtains.

"I spent all that money on chrome, I wanted people to see it," he said. "Plus, it runs cooler."

REAR AXLE AND DRIVE SHAFT

Katzke used the rear axle from the same '73 Ventura that supplied the subframe. The $20 cost made it $60 total for the frame and axle from the Ventura.

The drive shaft came from a 1984 Firebird.

"We found a Firebird upside down in the salvage yard," Katzke said. "I didn't think we'd find a drive shaft (that fit). I thought we would definitely have to shorten or lengthen it. I pulled out a wrench and yanked it off (the Firebird) myself and low and behold the thing fit in there just like it was made for it! Just a stroke of luck!"

The truck received a new windshield and wipers. The wipers came from a kit.

The finished custom tailgate.

FENDERS

The fenders gave Katzke one of his more difficult decisions. The existing metal fenders from the truck were in questionable shape, and there was no guarantee they would hold up in the long run.

"I took them to a body shop and it was going to cost $1,500 to get them done, but he couldn't guarantee they wouldn't rust later on because there was rust inside that he couldn't get at," Katzke said. "And I knew there were other trucks that had the same problem. So we went with fiberglass fenders and fiberglass running boards.

"When you're going to put $5,000-$6,000 into a paint job, and in five or six years it starts bubbling, that's not too good."

GAUGES, BRAKE PEDALS, RADIO, WIPERS, HEATER, ETC.

The 6-volt instrument cluster from the truck wouldn't work in the new 12-volt system, so Katzke transplanted the instrument cluster from the van. Ditto for the brake pedals.

"The van had suspended brake pedals and they were great, and they're free," Katzke said. "I got all

The "cotton candy" painting process begins.

The finished interior.

three pedals from the van: the emergency brake, brake and gas pedal."

A new radio was mounted on the ceiling of the cab and connected to four speakers. The electric wipers came from a kit. The heater came from another unlikely source.

"The AMCs used to have great heaters in them," Katzke said. "I salvaged a system from a '76 Pacer. I altered it to fit in the '46, which was quite a feat in itself, and it works fantastic."

The ashtray from the truck was cut out to make room for fresh air and air conditioning controls. "We have push buttons for vents and fresh air," he said.

WHEELS

The truck rides on 15-inch polished wheels on the back and 14-inchers on the front with Michelin tires.

"We didn't want it to just sit there. We got to thinking about the stance," Katzke said. "It's higher in the rear. When I was a kid we called that 'rake.' That seems to be the 'in' thing and I like the way it looks.

"I don't even know what make (the rims) are. A friend had them and we polished them up and I just liked the way they looked. That's part of the beauty of building your own car. Normal cars use normal stock wheels, but with hot rods you can put anything you want on them. It's all up to you."

The doors have power windows and hidden speakers, but no handles (inside or out).

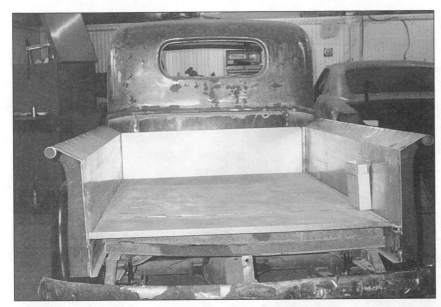

A custom, homemade box.

The tailgate was welded shut with a
new splash pan also welded in.

The taillights from a Chevy S10 were
frenched in, continuing the sleek,
rounded design for the truck box.

Outside and running.

POWER EQUIPMENT

Katzke's vehicle is loaded when it comes to electronic gadgetry. In additon to the power steering and power windows — which Katzke installed himself — stereo, and gas cap door, the Cotton Candy Express has power doors.

"We figured 'who wants door handles?'" Katzke said. "I have a push button on my key chain and the doors pop open electrically."

There are no door handles inside or out. There is a back-up switch hidden on the outside of the car that opens the doors, as well as push buttons inside under the dash for the driver and passengers. An emergency hook inside will also open the doors.

"It kind of blows people's minds when they walk up to the truck and I push one of the buttons in my pocket to let them look inside," Katzke said.

He also has a theft-prevention system integrated into the fuel pump.

"Somebody may try to steal it," Katzke said. "but they won't go far."

WINDSHIELD AND WINDOWS

Katzke installed new power windows from a kit and also put in a new crank-out two-piece windshield.

"It's really great having power windows in a 55-year-old vehicle," he said. "The windshield is great for fresh air – bugs and all."

Katzke elected to remove the steel frames around the windshield and windows.

"The '46 had ugly steel frames. You could paint it, but it would still look ugly," he said.

PAINT SCHEME

Since the truck was going to his wife, Bonnie, Katzke left the paint choices up to her. She also came up with the "Cotton Candy Express" moniker for the vehicle. "The name came first, and I picked it because when we were dating Paul called me 'Cotton Candy,'" Bonnie said. "I went with a raspberry that fades to pearl. Paul said he wasn't going to drive a pink truck, but I told him it would be raspberry."

The tailgate is home to the signature logo of the truck: A cartoon granny hanging out the window of a '46 Chevy pickup shaking a cane with Chevy "bow-tie" earrings flying in the breeze.

"We went to an artist and showed him the truck and I told him about my idea … and he took it from there," Bonnie said.

The black tonneau cover also has a design with a truck sitting atop a cone of cotton candy.

INTERIOR AND UPHOLSTERY

The interior features a clean look with a bench seat and gray/silver trimmed in raspberry.

"I wanted a silver interior, and I picked out the materials, but I pretty much left it up to the upholstery shop to design everything," Bonnie said. "We really wanted to keep the cab of the truck looking as much like the original '46 as we could. That's why we didn't chop it."

The Katzkes have collected dozens of trophies for their first street rod.

Paul complied with Bonnie's wish to have a bench seat in front by plucking a front seat from a 1973 Ford Maverick.

"At first it fit fine, but then we found out it didn't fit when the door panels were in," Paul said. "So we had to narrow it. We cut it in half and took out 3 inches and then re-mounted it."

TRUCK BED AND BACK END

Katzke initially planned to salvage the original bed and box, but those plans eventually changed.

"The bed, at first I thought it was decent until I got it home. Then I wasn't happy at all," he said.

Katzke decided to make his own box with a piece of sheet metal. A local steel fabricating company bent the corners for him. "That probably cost me $150, where if you buy one it's $1,200 or $1,300," Katzke said.

He then built a new license plate bracket, welded in a splash pan on the tailgate, welded the tailgate shut ("We weren't going to be hauling anything,") and frenched in some taillights from a Chevy S-10 pickup. The box's smooth, rounded look was aided by two straight pieces of exhaust pipe that were welded along the top edge of the box.

"It's all custom. It was all done very nicely and professionally," he said.

CHROME

Katzke admits he's a big fan of chrome, and he didn't skimp when it came time to put the finishing touches on his first street rod engine.

"We wanted the engine compartment to look good. We chromed just about everything you could chrome in the engine," he said. "You need sunglasses to sneak up on it."

One innovation Katzke was particularly proud of was his makeshift chrome firewall and fender wells.

"The original firewall had a lot of holes in it, so we found an old stainless steel door off the back door of a semi," he said. "We made that into the firewall. Now it looks like a mirror."

THE EXPENSE ACCOUNT

Katzke can sympathize with fellow hot rodders who find their budget difficult to stick to. Despite being an experienced car guy — he formerly worked for *Old Cars Weekly* magazine — he saw his budget plan unravel in a big way.

An overhead view of the finished product.

"That was one of the biggest shocks," he admits. "I've built cars and consider myself well-versed. I thought it would take $7,000 to $10,000, but halfway through I was $5,000 over already. Then I thought 'Gosh, this is getting to be too much,' but then I just said damn the torpedoes and full speed ahead. I just decided I was going to build the best car I could. That's why it took me 7 years to finish it — it took me that long to get the money together."

GARAGE AND EQUIPMENT

Katzke started his project in an unheated barn, but finished in a more accommodating eight-car heated garage. He insists his work area is no commercial garage, however.

"I've got a torch, but nothing fancy, just the average tools most car guys have," he said. "Mostly I'm fortunate to have some friends with some extreme mechanical abilities that bail me out occasionally. And I try to bail them out when I can."

TOUGHEST OBSTACLES

"The down part was whenever I started adding up the receipts to see how much we spent," Katzke joked. "That was the only thing I could see."

BIGGEST SURPRISES

The Ventura subframe worked out well overall, but it was still the source of many man hours.

"One of the biggest hurdles that came along was mounting the front of the vehicle to the '73 frame," Katzke said. "There were no mounts on the frame to mount the fenders, radiator shell — nothing. All that had to be fabricated. That came as a surprise to me. It was a bigger project than I was anticipating."

BIGGEST CHANGES ALONG THE WAY

Katzke made one particularly big change during the building process — he originally planned to build up two trucks, but that plan went out the window when the bill for the Cotton Candy Express started to mount.

"I just decided to pour all my money into one truck and make it the best that I could," he said.

REGRETS

If he could do everything over again, Katzke said the only part of the truck he would change would be the door hinges.

"I might still make the door hinges hidden," he said. "I left the '46 hinges, because I wanted to keep kind of an antique look."

THE FUTURE

Since Paul now has his own show truck, the couple stays plenty busy, traveling from show to show, during the summer months. "I take my truck and my wife takes hers," he said. "Sometimes we're even in the same class. She tells me I can't beat her, because even if I win, I'm beating my own truck."

In the past six years, the couple have logged about 17,000 miles on the Cotton Candy Express. "We drive it everywhere," he said. "We never trailer it."

ADVICE TO OTHER BUILDERS

Katzke knew that he loved building and rebuilding stock automobiles before he ever began his first custom car. It didn't take him long to realize he loved working on hot rods even more.

He insists it was that enthusiasm for the work and single-mindedness to see the project through to the end that made his first hot rodding effort a success.

"You know, we take the '46 to a lot of shows, and we always get one to three people who come up and tell me they have a truck like mine and ask a lot of questions and say 'I can't find this part, I can't find that part,'" Katzke said. "And I always hand out my card and tell them I can help them out finding parts. In all this time, only one person has actually ever called me. You get a lot of big talkers.

"It takes determination. You really have to want it. If you're a smoker and you try to quit, you really have to want to quit. Same thing if you're a drinker. You really have to want to quit.

"Talk is cheap. You have to really want to get out there every night and work on it. The main thing is determination."

Appendix A

Painting defects recognition, prevention, corrections

Despite careful preparation, modern application technology and the use of sophisticated paint systems, defects can never be completely ruled out in vehicle refinishing. However, a professional body shop today cannot afford to produce bad-quality results. And repairing a defect often takes a great deal of time and effort.

What are the causes? What mistakes were made? Spies Hecker has compiled the most frequent defects a painter encounters into this easy-to-use reference.

It is only when a defect has been correctly identified that causes be eliminated and the damage to the painted object efficiently repaired.

> **All paint companies have technical assistance available. If any of the flaws on the following pages show up in your paint work, contact your local paint supplier.**

DIRT AND DUST

DEFINITION

- Particles protruding from the surface of the coat.

CAUSE

- The vehicle surface was not effectively cleaned before paint application.

- The air filters need replacing.

- The pressure in the spray booth was too low.

- The painters were wearing unsuitable clothing.

PREVENTION

- Before painting ensure the vehicle surface has been properly cleaned with a tack cloth.

- Check the filters regularly.

- Wear overalls that are free of lint.

- Make sure the spray booth is maintained in a clean condition.

REMEDY

- Lightly sand and polish the affected area.

- If this is unsuccessful, sand the entire area, clean with silicone remover and respray.

STAINS (METALLICS)

DEFINITION

- Discolored patches on metallic top coats (such as blotch at left in photo).

CAUSE

- Areas of primer surfacer or putty were sanded.
- Too much hardener was used in polyester putty.

PREVENTION

- Apply a sealer coat on the sanded-through areas.
- Avoid too much hardener in polyester putty.

REMEDY

- Sand the entire area when it has dried through, clean with silicone remover and respray.
- If too much hardener was used in polyester putty, seal with spray polyester and reapply the paint system.

RUNS OR SAGS

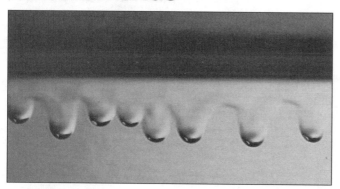

DEFINITION

- Paint runs on vertical body parts.

CAUSE

- Uneven paint application.
- The spraying viscosity was incorrect.
- Unsuitable thinners were used.

- Air, material or ambient temperature was too low.
- Film thicknesses were too high.
- Defective spray gun (nozzle).
- Intermediate flash-off time was too short.

PREVENTION

- Warm object and paint up to room temperature of 20 degrees C / 68 degrees F.
- Ensure that the spray gun is in good working order. Follow application recommendations in technical data sheets.

REMEDY

- After the paint has hardened thoroughly, sand the runs flat, lightly sand the entire area, if necessary allow to dry, clean with silicone remover and respray.
- With smaller defects, polish the affected area after sanding.

PORES / PIN HOLES

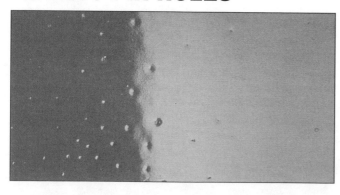

DEFINITION

- Pin-prick-sized holes as deep as the surfacer coat.

CAUSE

- Excessive film thicknesses in conjunction with forced drying.
- Pores in the putty surface were not filled.

PREVENTION

- Apply surfacer at normal film thicknesses.
- Keep to the recommended flash-off times.

REMEDY

- Allow top coat to dry through, then sand affected areas, clean with silicone remover, seal with a two-pack primer surfacer and respray.
- In severe cases sand down the top coat completely and reapply the entire paint system.

SOLVENT POPPING

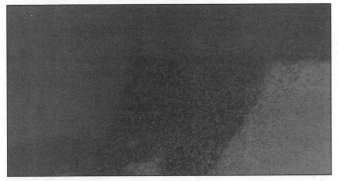

- Spray viscosity was not correct.
- Unsuitable hardener or reducer was used.

PREVENTION

- Apply normal film thicknesses.
- Keep to correct flash-off times.
- Use spray viscosity, hardeners and reducers given in the technical data sheet.

DEFINITION

- Small bubbles and pop marks in the top coat.

CAUSE

- Paint was applied at excessive film thicknesses.
- Top coat was not allowed to flash off long enough before low baking.

REMEDY

- Allow to dry through, then sand the affected areas, clean with silicone remover, seal any fine pores with two-pack acrylic primer surfacer and respray.
- Where popping is more extensive, sand down top coat completely and reapply paint system.

CRATERING / FISH EYES

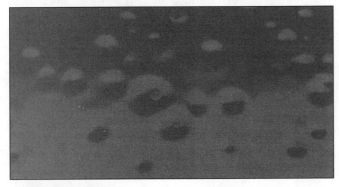

PREVENTION

- Check that regular maintenance is carried out on the air lines.
- Ensure that the filter is changed regularly (secondary filter about once a year, primary filter every three months).
- Clean surfaces properly with silicone remover before repairing and refinishing.

DEFINITION

- Crater-like depressions with raised edges.

CAUSE

- Substrate was not thoroughly cleaned with silicone remover.
- Air supply was contaminated with oil or water.
- Ceiling filter does not meet the requirements.

REMEDY

- Sand, clean with silicone remover and reapply top coat.

EDGE MAPPING

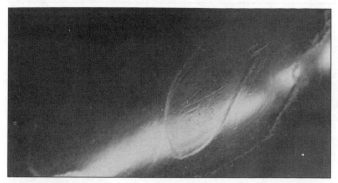

DEFINITION

• Ringing in the top coat around repairs.

CAUSE

• Sanded area not smoothly blended into old finish.

• Putty and surfacer were applied on top of elastic factory finishes.

• Surfacer was not allowed to dry through before being sanded and recoated.

• The substrate was not fully cured.

• Preparatory material applied at excessive film thicknesses and not allowed to dry properly.

PREVENTION

• Carry out a solvent test on the exposed paint layers (elastic/hard).

• Only apply putty on bare metal.

• With elastic factory finishes, apply surfacer to the entire area.

REMEDY

• After the top coat has dried thoroughly, sand and polish damaged area, if necessary seal with primer surfacer, and respray.

PORES IN SURFACER COAT

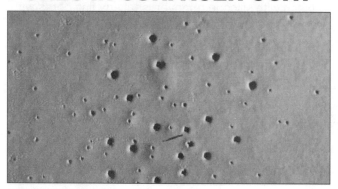

DEFINITION

• Small, pin-hole-like depressions.

CAUSE

• Spray viscosity was too high.

• Unsuitable hardener was used, ea. fast hardener at high temperatures.

• Excessive film thicknesses.

PREVENTION

• Follow the application recommendations in the technical data sheet.

• Choose the correct hardener for the ambient temperature.

• Apply surfacer at the recommended film thicknesses.

REMEDY

• Sand down and reapply paint system.

SANDING MARKS

DEFINITION

• Scratches with swollen edges.

CAUSE

• The abrasive paper used to sand the putty or surfacer was too coarse.

• The surfacer was not allowed to dry sufficiently before recoating.

PREVENTION

- Use the recommended abrasive paper for sanding: Putty: first sanding P 180, final sanding P 320. Surfacer: dry P 400, wet P 800.
- Follow instructions for drying the surfacer given in the technical data sheet.

REMEDY

- When the top coat has dried through, finely sand and polish the affected area.
- For deeper marks, sand and reapply top coat.

SPECKS (METALLICS)

DEFINITION

- Points protruding from the paint film.

CAUSE

- Metallic base coat was not applied wet enough for the metallic particles to settle into the paint.

- The clear coat was not able to cover these vertical particles.

PREVENTION

- Apply the base coat in accordance with the instructions in the technical data sheet.
- Maintain the correct distance between spray gun and object (approximately 8 inches).

REMEDY

- Allow clear coat to dry, lightly sand with P 800, clean with silicone remover and reapply clear coat.

SOLVENT ATTACK / PICK-UP / RIPPLING

DEFINITION

- Lifting/wrinkling of the paint surface.

CAUSE

- Substrate was not fully cured or is solvent-sensitive.
- Areas where clear coat was sanded through to base coat were not sealed with a suitable primer surfacer.
- Unsuitable substrate (TPA) and nitrocellulose paints.

- Unsuitable priming materials, top coats or reducers were used.

PREVENTION

- Carry out solvent test on problematic substrates.
- On difficult substrates apply several thin coats of two-pack primer surfacer and allow longer flash-off times.

REMEDY

- Allow to dry through, completely remove both the wrinkled top coat and the contaminated substrate and reapply the paint system.
- Before applying the top coat, sand the entire area.

BLISTERING

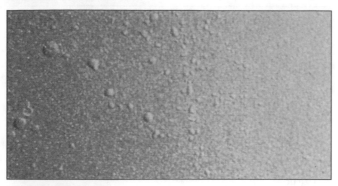

DEFINITION

- Small raised dots in the surface.

CAUSE

- Moisture was absorbed by the substrate.

- Areas to be painted were not allowed to dry completely after wet sanding (particularly a problem with polyester products). Air humidity before painting was too high.

- Temperature fluctuation led to condensation.

- Pores/pin holes in the substrate were not sanded out.

- Polyester products were not sealed.

PREVENTION

- Only dry sand polyester products and apply sealer coat.

- Carefully sand out or apply more putty to fill pin holes.

- Check the air humidity regularly.

REMEDY

- Sand down the affected area completely, sand the remaining surface well, clean with silicone remover, apply primer surfacer and then top coat.

DIE BACK / MATTING / GLOSS

DEFINITION

- Loss of gloss on the top coat.

CAUSE

- Surfacer was not allowed to dry sufficiently.

- Unsuitable reducers were used, causing the substrate to dissolve.

- Contaminated hardener was used.

- Excessive film build of top coat.

PREVENTION

- Keep to the drying times given in the technical data sheets.

- Use only the recommended reducers.

- Close hardener cans firmly after use to ensure proper seal.

- Apply top coat as per technical data sheets.

REMEDY

- After drying, polish the affected area to remove the matting, or lightly sand the entire surface, clean with silicone remover and respray.

CRATERING IN THE SURFACER

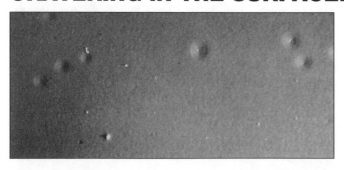

DEFINITION

- Crater-like depressions with raised edges.

CAUSE

- Substrate was not sufficiently cleaned with silicone remover.

- Air supply contaminated with oil or water (defective oil and water separator in air line).

PREVENTION

- Thoroughly clean the substrate with silicone remover.

- Ensure that regular maintenance is carried out on the air lines.

REMEDY

- Allow to dry and then sand out the cratering.
- Clean the entire area and reapply surfacer.

WATER MARKS

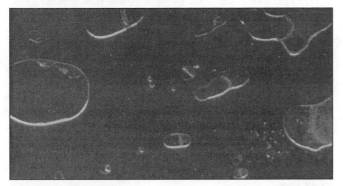

DEFINITION

- Round marks on the paint surface.

CAUSE

- Water droplets evaporated off fresh paint work which is not fully dry; this is mainly a problem on horizontal surfaces.

PREVENTION

- Keep to the drying times given in the technical data sheets.

REMEDY

- Where isolated marking has occurred, lightly sand with P 1000 and then polish.
- With severe contamination, sand the area well, clean with silicone remover and respray.

ORANGE PEEL

DEFINITION

- Uneven surface formation resembling orange peel.

CAUSE

- Spray viscosity was too high.
- Fast reducers/hardeners were used.

- Temperature in the spray booth was too high.
- Distance between spray nozzle and object was too great, paint was applied too dry.

PREVENTION

- Set the spray booth temperature at approximately 20 degrees C / 68 degrees F.
- Use a suitable reducer hardener for the particular repair.
- Check the paint viscosity with a DIN viscosity cup.
- Maintain a spraying distance of approximately eight inches.

REMEDY

- Sand down the uneven surface and respray.

CORROSION / RUSTING

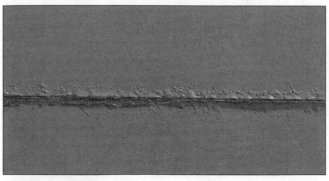

DEFINITION

- Mechanical damage with rusting under the paint film.

CAUSE

- Stone chipping combined with road salt and moisture.

- Moisture on bare metal prior to priming.

PREVENTION

- Thoroughly clean and blow off bare metal prior to priming.

REMEDY

- Sand paint down to the metal.

- Refinish with one-pack corrosion primer, then the usual surfacer and top coat.

STAINING

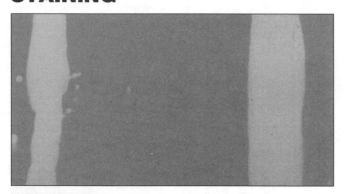

DEFINITION

- Occasional stains on the finish.

CAUSE

- Contamination of the surface by chemically reactive materials such as chalk, cement dust, strong detergent cleaners and bird droppings.

REMEDY

- In most cases gloss can be restored by polishing.

- If this is not successful, sand the area, clean with silicone remover and respray.

- If necessary, sand down and reapply the paint system.

WATER BLISTERS

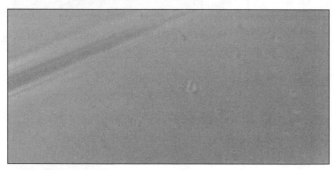

DEFINITION

- Medium-sized blisters in the top coat.

CAUSE

- Residues of sanding water which have collected in corners, edges and under moldings. Contaminated air supply.

PREVENTION

- Blow clean air into recesses after sanding to check they are dry. Always remove add-on parts if possible.

- Check regularly that oil and water separator on compressed air line is working efficiently.

REMEDY

- For light contamination, sand damaged area and then polish.

- Where contamination is more severe, sand and respray.

MOTTLING / STRIPING

DEFINITION

• Uneven color or special effect formation.

CAUSE

• Defective spray gun (nozzle).

• Fluctuating air pressure, unsuitable reducer, incorrect spraying technique, incorrect spraying viscosity.

PREVENTION

• Use mixing stick or DIN viscosity cup to set spraying viscosity. Ensure spray guns are maintained regularly. Keep spray gun parallel to object while spraying at a distance of approximately 8 inches. Follow closely the application recommendations in the technical data sheets.

REMEDY

• Allow to dry thoroughly then sand surface and re-spray with top coat system.

PEELING PROBLEMS WITH POLYESTER MATERIAL

DEFINITION

• Areas of polyester putty peeling off.

CAUSE

• Substrate was not carefully prepared.

• Unsuitable polyester putty was used.

• Infra-red drying was not carried out correctly.

PREVENTION

• The substrate must be cleaned and sanded thoroughly. Before applying polyester putty, carefully read the technical data sheet.

• Use putties and primers that are recommended for galvanized substrates.

• Follow the manufacturer's instructions for infra-red drying.

REMEDY

• Sand the defective paint work well, then repair and refinish with suitable materials.

LOW HIDING POWER / OPACITY

DEFINITION

• Uneven color of finish.

CAUSE

• Wrong surfacer used for three-stage systems. Insufficient application of top coat.

PREVENTION

• Ensure top coats are applied at recommended film thicknesses. With low opacity colors, use the surfacer stipulated. Apply a neutral-colored primer surfacer.

REMEDY

• Sand and respray.

POLISHING MARKS

DEFINITION

- Round polishing marks of various sizes with reduced gloss or an uneven surface that was polished through.

CAUSE

- Unsuitable polishing compound was used. The surface was uneven, leading to high spots being polished through. Polishing was carried out before the top coat was dried through.

PREVENTION

- Use suitable polishing compounds and equipment. Check that the top coat is completely dry before polishing.

REMEDY

- Ensure that the top coat is completely dry and then repolish. If affected areas are still visible, sand and respray.

Appendix B

Resources

3M
3M Center Building 223-6N-01
St Paul, MN 55144
http://www.mmm.com

A & M SoffSeal Inc.
104 May Drive
Harrison OH 45030
http://www.soffseal.com

A.C.E. Sand Blasting Equipment
897 South Washington PMB 232
Holland, MI 49423

Advanced Plating
955 East Trinity Lane
Nashville, TN 37207
http://www.advancedplating.com

AFCO Hot Rod Products
P.O. Box 548
Booneville, IN 47601
http://www.hotrodafco.com

Affordable Street Rods
1220 Van Buren
Great Bend, KS 67530
http://www.affordablestreetrods.com

Air Ride Technologies Inc.
2762 Cathy Drive
Jasper, IN 47546

Alumicraft Street Road Grilles
308 South Fourth St.
Bellwood, PA 16617
http://www.alumicraft.com

American Autowire
150 Heller Place #17W
Bellmawr NJ 08031

American Racing Custom Wheels
19067 South Reyes Ave.
Rancho Dominguez, CA 90221
http://www.americanracing.com

American Stamping
8650 Mid-South Drive
Oilve Branch, MS 38654

Auto Chic
P.O. Box 6181
West Caldwell, NJ 07007
http://www.liquidglass.com

Auto Meter Products
413 West Elm St
Sycamor, IL 60178
http://www.autometer.com

Autoweek
1400 Woodbridge Ave.
Detroit, MI 48207
http://www.autoweek.com

B & M Racing & Performance Products
9142 Independence Ave.
Chatsworth, CA 91311
http://www.bmracing.com

Backyard Buddy Corp.
140 Dana St
Warren, OH 44483
http://www.backyardbuddy.com

Ball's Rod & Kustom
10121 North State Road 13
Syracuse, IN 46567
http://www.ballsrodandkustom.com

Beugler Stripers
3667 Tracy St.
Los Angeles, CA 90039
http://www.beugler.com

B F Goodrich Tires
One Parkway South
Greenville, SC 29602
http://www.bfgoodrichtires.com

Billet Specialties Inc.
340 Shore Drive
Burr Ridge, IL 60521
http://billetspecialties.com

Bob Drake Reproductions Inc.
1899 NW Hawthorne Ave.
Grants Pass, OR 97526
http://www.bobdrake.com

Borgeson Universal Co. Inc.
187 Commercial Blvd.
Torrington, CT 06790
http://www.borgeson.com

Brite Ideas
1420 Shell Flower Drive
Brandon, FL 33571

Buckaroo Communications Inc.
12434 Prescilla Road
Camarillo, CA 93012
http://wwwsuperrod.com
http://www.streetrodbuilder.com

Busch Enterprises Inc.
908 Cochran St.
Statesville, NC 28677

California Car Cover Co.
9525 DeSoto Ave.
Chatsworth, CA 913111
http://www.calcarduster.com

Chevrolet Motor Division
100 Renaissance Center
Detroit, MI 48265
http://www.chevrolet.com

City Glass & Upholstery
1943 Tacoma Ave. South
Tacoma, WA 98402
http://www.cityglass.net/Automobiles.html

Classic Enterprises
P.O. Box 1162
Pleasantville, NJ 08232
http://www.classicenterprises.com

Coker Tire
1317 Chestnut St.
Chattanooga, TN 37402
http://www.coker.com

Colorado Custom
2421 International
Ft. Collins, CO 80524
http://www.coloradocustom.com

Crossfire Mfg.
P.O. Box 263
Sharpsville, PA 16150

Custom Rodtronics
22105 Westwind Dr.
Elkhorn, NE 68022

C.W.Moss Ford Parts Inc.
402 West Chapman Ave.
Orange CA 92866
http://www.cwmoss.com

Dakota Digital
3421 West Hovland Ave.
Sioux Falls, SD 57107
http://www.dakotadigital.com

Danny's Rod Shop
1853 Old State Rt. 28
Goshen, OH 45122

Denver Specialty Center
7801 East Colfax
Denver, CO 80220

Design Engineering Inc.
36960 Detroit Road
Avon, OH 44011

Downs Mfg.
715 North Main St.
Lawton, MI 49065

DuPont Automotive Finishes
312 Center St
Farmington, MO 63640
http://www.dupont.com/finishes

Eagle One
5927 Landau Ct.
Carlsbad, CA 92008
http://www.eagleone.com

Earl's Performance Products
189 West Victoria St.
Long Beach, CA 90805
http://www.earlsperformance.com

Eaton Detroit Spring Inc.
1555 Michigan
Detoit, MI 48216
http://www.eatonsprings.com

Edelbrock
2700 California Ave.
Torrance, CA 90503
http://www.edelbrock.com

Emgee/Clean Tools
10 Plaza Drive
Westmont, IL 60559
http://www.emgee@mcs.net

Engineered Components Inc.
P.O. Box 841
Vernon, CT 06066

Fatman Fabrications Inc.
8621-C Fairview Road Hwy 218
Charlotte, NC 28227-7619
http://www.fatmanfab.com

Flaming River Industries Inc.
800 Poertner Drive
Berea, OH 44017
http://www.flamingriver.com

Ford Racing
14555 Rotunda Drive Suite 131
Dearborn, MI 48120
http://www.fordracing.com

GM Performance Parts
6200 Grand Pointe Drive
Grand Blanc, MI 48439
http://www.gmgoodwrench.com

Gibbon Fiberglass Reproductions
132 Industrial Way
Darlington, SC 29532
http://www.gibbonfiberglass.com

Godman Hi-Performance
5255 Elmore Road
Memphis, TN 38134
http://www.godmanhiperformance.com

Goldcoast Coating
19 Aviador Unit A
Camarillo, CA 93010

Goldeez Hot Rod Products
400 Easton Drive Suite 1
Bakersfield, CA 93309
http://www.goldeez.com

Goodyear Tire
1144 East Market St.
Akron, OH 44316
http://www.goodyear.com

Hagan Street Rod Necessities
2179 Joanne Drive #4
Carson City, NV 89701
http://www.haganstreetrods.com

Haneline Products Co
P.O. Box 430
Morongo Valley, CA 92256

Haywire Inc.
1415 Prairie View Road
Joplin, MO 64804
http://www.haywireinc.com

Heidt's Hot Rod Shop
1345 North Old Rand Road
Wauconda, IL 60084

Hercules Motor Car Co.
2502 North 70th St.
Tampa, FL 33619
http://www.herculesmotorcarcompany.com

Holley Performance Products
1801 Russellville Road
Bowling Green, KY 42102
http://www.holley.com

Hotrod Hotline
10400 Overland Road #402
Boise, ID 83709
http://www.hotrodhotline.com

House of Kolor/Valspar
210 Crosby St.
Picayune, MS 39466
http://www.houseofkolor.com

Howron Industries
1915 Laurelwood Drive
Denton, TX 76201

HPC
550 West 3615 South
Salt Lake City, UT 84115
http://www.hpcoatings.com

Inland Empire Driveline
4035 East Guasti Road #302
Ontario, CA 91761

Insulshield Technologies
207 Cushing St.
Hingham, MA 02043
http://www.insulshield.net

Interiors by Shannon
907 Overhill Drive
Alexander City, AL 35010
http://www.interiorsbyshannon.com

Jake's Pinstriping
8309 Hwy 80 West
Ft Worth, TX 76116
http://www.jakespinstriping.com

Jet Hot Coatings Division MCCI
55 East Front St.
Bridgeport, PA 19405
http://www.jethot1.com

Juliano's Interior Products
321 Talcotteville Road
Vernon, CT 06066
http://www.julianos.com

Kemps Rod and Restoration, Inc.
636 Industrial Park Drive
Iron Mountain, MI 49801
http://www.exploringthenorth.com/kemp/rods.html

Kimberly-Clark/Scott DIY Business
300 Chesterfield Center Suite 200
Chesterfield, MO 63017

KWIKLIFT INC.
610 North Walnut
Broken Arrow, OK 74012
http://www.kwiklift.com

Kwik Poly
P.O. Box 12330
O'Fallon, MO 63366

Lokar Inc.
10924 Murdock Drive
Knoxville, TN 37932

Made For You Products
P.O. Box 720700
Pinon Hills, CA 92372
http://www.made4uproducts.com

McGard Inc.
3875 California Road
Orchard Park, NY 14127
http://www.mcgard.com

Meguiar's Inc.
17991 Mitchell St.
Irvine, CA 92614
http://www.meguiars.com

Miller Electric
1635 West Spencer St.
Appleton WI 54914

Mr. Gasket Co.
10601 Memphis Ave. #12
Cleveland, OH 44144
http://www.mrgasket.com

Mullins Steering Gears
2876 Sweetwater Ave. #2
Lake Havasu City, AZ 86406
http://www.mullinssteeringgears.com

Old Chicago Street Rods
16169 SE 106
Clackamas, OR 97015

Outlaw Performance Inc.
P.O. Box 550 Rt. 380 Nelson
Avonmore, PA 15618
http://www.outlawrods.com

Parr Automotive
4933 NW 10th St
Oklahoma City, OK 73127
http://www.parrautomotive.com

P-Ayr Products
719 Delaware St.
Leavanworth, KS 66048
http://www.payr.com

Pete & Jakes Hot Rod Parts
401 Legend Lane
Peculiar, MO 64078
http://www.peteandjakes.com

Powermaster
2401 Dutch Valley Road
Knoxville, TN 37918
http://www.powermastermotorsports.com

PPG Industries Inc.
19699 Progress Drive
Strongsville, OH 44136
http://www.ppg.com

Pro-Blend Motorsports
830 Manly St.
Winston Salem, NC 27101

RB's Obsolete Auto
7711 Lake Ballinger Way
Edmonds, WA 98026
http://www.rbsobsolete.com

Richmond Gear
1208 Old Norris Road
Liberty, SC 29657

Rocky Hinge Co.
1720 Wilson Ave.
Girard, OH 44420

Rod Doors
PO box 2160
Chico, CA 95927
http://www.roddoors.com

Ron Francis Wire Works
167 Keystone Road
Chester, PA 19013
http://www.wire-works.com

Sanderson Street Rod Headers
517 Railroad Ave.
San Francisco, CA 94080
http://www.sandersonheaders.com

Sharp Enterprises
1005 Cole St.
Laclede. MO 64651

Showtime Automobile Accessories
899 North Market St.
Selinsgrove, PA 17870

Sneed Robinson & Gerber Inc.
6645 Stage Road
Bartlett, TN 38134
http://www.sneedcompanies.com

Southern Rods & Parts Inc.
2125 Airport Road
Greer, SC 29650
http://www.southernrods.com

Springfield Street Rod
219 Buxton
Springfield, OH 45505
http://www.springfieldstreetrods.com

Stewart Warner Instruments
200 Howard Ave. Bldg. 250
Des Plaines, IL 60018
http://www.stewartwarner.com

Stinger by Axe Equipment
Hwy 177 North/P.O. Box 296
Council Grove, KS 66846
http://www.stingerlifts.com

Street Rod Digital
14241 NE Woodinville-Duvall Road #101
Woodinville, WA 98072
http://www.streetroddigital.com

Street & Performance Inc.
Rt 5 #1 Hot Rod Lane
Mena, AR 71953
http://www.hotrodlane.cc

Street Rodder Magazine
2400 East Katella St.
Anaheim, CA 92806
http://www.streetrodderweb.com

Street Rods by Michael
120 Deery St.
Shelbyville, TN 37160
http://www.srbymichael.com

TD Performance
16410 Manning Way
Cerritos, CA 90703
http://www.tdperformance.com

TL Rod and Custom
122 Deery St.
Shelbyville, TN 37160
http://www.tlrodandcustom.com

Tea's Design
2038 15th St. NW
Rochester, MN 55901
http://www.teasdesign.com

The Eastwood Company
580 Lancaster Ave. P.O. Box 296
Malvern, PA 19355
http://www.eastwoodcompany.com

The Lincoln Electric Co
22801 St. Clair Ave.
Cleveland, OH 44117
http://www.lincolnelectric.com

The Wheel Tough Co.
P.O. Box 10073
Terre Haute, IN 47801
http://www.wheeltough.com

Total Cost Involved Engineering Inc.
1416 West Brooks St.
Ontario, CA 91762

Total Performance Inc.
400 South Orchard St Rt. 5
Wallingford, CT 06492
http://www.tperformance.com

TPI Performance Transmissions
231 S. Lindberg
Griffith, IN 46319
http://www.tpiperformace.com

Ultra Tek
82 Cannas Ct.
Cheektowaga, NY 14227

VDO Performance Instruments
188 Brooke Road
Winchester, VA 22603
http://vdona.com

Valley Auto Accessories
1554 E. 1333rd Lane
Flower, IL 62338

Village Buffing
902 East 22 St.
Kannapolis, NC 28083

Vintage Air Inc.
10305 IH 35 North
San Antonio, TX 78209
http://www.vintageair.com

Visibolts
7131 Hickory Lane
Waunakee, WI 53597
http://www.visibolts.com

Walker Radiator Works
694 Marshall Ave.
Memphis, TN 38103
http://www.hotrodsworldwide.com/catalogs/walker.htm

Warren Motorsports
7065 West Ann Rd #130-207
Las Vegas, NV 89130
http://www.warren-motorsports.com

Watson's Street Works Rod & Custom
P.O. Box 270
Bozrah, CT 06334
www.watsons-streetworks.com

Weld Wheel Industries Inc.
933 Mulberry St.
Kansas City, MO 64101
http://weldracing.com

Wescott's Auto Restyling
19701 SE Hwy. 212
Boring, OR 97009
http://www.wescottsauto.com

William's Welding
14770 Cooks Mills Road
Humboldt, IL 61931

Yearwood Speed & Custom
6830 Gateway East
El Paso, TX 79915
http://www.yearwood.com

Yogi's Inc.
PO Box 68
Calamus, IA 52729
http://www.yogisinc.com

Zoops Products Inc.
931 East Lincoln St.
Banning, CA 92220
http://www.zoops.com

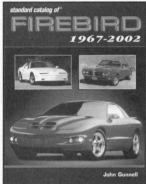

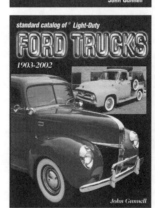
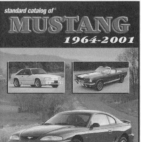
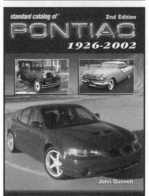

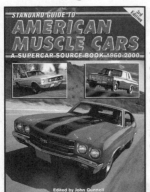
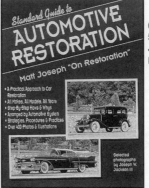

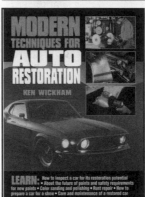
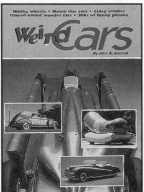

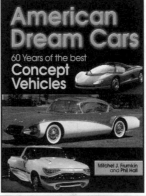